HARRIS FRANKLIN RALL is Professor of
Systematic Theology, Garrett Biblical Institute.
He was graduated from the University of Iowa
with Phi Beta Kappa honors, secured his A.M.
and B.D. degrees from Yale University and,
after serving as a fellow of Yale at both the
University of Berlin and the University of
Halle-Wittenberg, was awarded the degrees of
A.M. and Ph.D. by the latter institution.

In 1900 he was ordained a Methodist minister
and served as pastor of Trinity Church, New
Haven, and First Church, Baltimore. In 1910
he became President of Iliff School of Theology, Denver. From this position he went
to Garrett Biblical Institute where he has been
for more than a quarter of a century.

Dr. Rall's pen has rarely been idle. A fre-
quent contributor to leading religious period-
icals he is also author of several books. Among
these are: SOCIAL MINISTRY, A WORKING FAITH,
LIFE OF JESUS, TEACHINGS OF JESUS, MODERN PRE-
MILLENNIALISM AND THE CHRISTIAN HOPE, THE
COMING KINGDOM, THE MEANING OF GOD, CHRIS-
TIANITY TODAY, BEHAVIORISM—A BATTLE LINE,
CONTEMPORARY AMERICAN THEOLOGY, A FAITH
FOR TODAY and RELIGION AND PUBLIC AFFAIRS.
His volume CHRISTIANITY—AN INQUIRY INTO ITS
NATURE AND TRUTH was recently awarded the
$15,000 Fiftieth Anniversary Bross Prize, next
to the Nobel award one of the richest literary
prizes in the world.

A Faith for Today

HARRIS FRANKLIN RALL

ABINGDON-COKESBURY PRESS

NEW YORK • **NASHVILLE**

RALL
A FAITH FOR TODAY

Copyright, 1936, by
HARRIS FRANKLIN RALL

Wartime Books

*Wartime shortage of pulp, manpower, and transportation has
produced a severe shortage of paper. In compliance with orders
of the War Production Board, wartime books are printed on
lighter-weight paper. This reduces thickness and weight. New
books have more words to the page and smaller margins. This reduces the number of pages without reducing reading content.*

*Thinner books save paper, critical copper, and other metals.
They help also to avoid wartime increases in book prices.
Wartime books appear to be smaller, but their content has not
been cut. They are complete. The only change is in appearance.*

Printed in the United States of America

TO

M. S. J. R.

M. E. R.

CONTENTS

A FOREWORD

THIS book is written for men who want a faith by which to live, who wish to hold it intelligently, who want to face honestly all the facts bearing upon the matter, and then with equal honesty ask what such a faith means for life.

The reasons for such a discussion at this time are obvious. On the one hand is the growing realization of the need of such a faith, without which life becomes unmeaning for the individual and impossible for society. On the other hand there is, among religious folk, widespread confusion and question, and among others a rather common impression that modern knowledge has made faith impossible. The situation is not met by piecemeal discussions of science and religion, or of religion and social problems, or of religion and the new psychology; nor is it enough that scholars should consider one problem or another in learned studies. What is needed is a systematic inquiry into the religious problem for the common man, and a setting forth of a valid and commanding faith. A double conviction underlies these chapters: that religion is every man's concern because it is the supreme interest of life, and that every man has a right to an honest treatment of its problems and a convincing statement of its principles.

This situation indicates the method of procedure here followed: (1) to take what is highest in those insights of faith in which the funded experiences of the race have come to us; (2) to face the questions which are raised by modern thought and modern conditions of life; (3) to seek any enlargement of vision or correction of error which may come through the growing knowledge of the race; (4) to ask what such a faith brings to our need and what it demands of our life. For me the supreme insight of faith is that which has come to our race through Jesus of Nazareth. But this insight is not a system of theology which shuts off inquiry; it is, rather, a summons to fare forth on the road of experiment and adventurous search, with faith in a living God and a growing knowledge of the truth. Empiricism and faith here go together, the spirit of science and the spirit of religion, not as competitors but as akin to each other.

As to form, my one desire is, in Robert Louis Stevenson's phrase, "to say out what I mean about life, and man, and God in fair and square human language." There are certain great obstacles to fruitful religious inquiry: the technical language of the theologians, the traditional phrases of religion worn smooth and become meaningless with long usage, the threshing of old straw in the form of religious issues that have no value for present-day life, and the desire to defend a system rather than discover the truth. It has, therefore, been my effort to write in plainest English, using the language of that everyday world where religion belongs, to include no theme merely because it belongs to the tradition of the Church, and to avoid no question because it is difficult or dangerous to the religious view.

For something over twenty years I have been discussing religion with my students in theological halls whose east windows look out on the broad expanse of

Lake Michigan, whose west windows front one of the busiest thoroughfares on this continent, whose seat is a university campus, and whose tower bears the symbol of the cross. Perhaps this may fairly be taken to represent in fourfold aspect the faith that is here set forth: a faith that looks out on the world of nature and makes room for its order, its beauty, its tragic aspects, and for that science which sums up our knowledge concerning it; a faith that looks out upon life, to gain wisdom from its experiences, to test conclusions by its experiments, to bring to it the supreme demand and the saving help of the Eternal; a faith that hides in no cloister but welcomes all inquiry and all knowledge, and desires no God but the God of truth; and, finally, a faith which finds the meaning of all nature and life and learning in the eternal God, and the revelation of that God in Jesus Christ.

HARRIS FRANKLIN RALL.

Garrett Biblical Institute,
Northwestern University Campus,
Evanston, Illinois.

I

THE MEANING OF FAITH

I. The Loss of Faith

Professor R. A. Millikan, the physicist, pointed out a few years ago that the well-being of humanity rested upon two pillars. One is science, "belief in the spirit and method of Galileo, of Newton, of Faraday, and of the other great builders of this modern scientific age." Through science we understand and rule our physical world, and make its forces serve us. But, he declared, "The most important thing in the world is a belief in the reality of moral and spiritual values. It was because we lost that belief that the World War came, and if we do not find a way to regain and strengthen that belief, then science is of no value."

In large areas today religious faith has disappeared. Some would ascribe this to science. "Once," they say, "men did not have knowledge; then they believed in God and angels and evil spirits, and they depended upon God for help. Now we know. Instead of the guesses of religion we have the facts of science; we observe and demonstrate by experiment. That is the only real knowledge, the world of science is the only real world, and the help that science gives us is the only real help. We do not pray God to avert an epidemic; we look for the germ. We do not ask God for rain; we learn about dry farming or plan for irrigation or wait for a better season."

Another reason for loss of faith lies in the practical

materialism of our age. Materialism as a theory holds that there is nothing real except matter; among thinking men that theory is dead. But materialism as a philosophy of life is very much alive. It rests upon the belief that the wealth of this world consists of things, and that to possess enough of things, or of the money that will command them, is the sure road to happiness. Never did the world of things offer so much attraction to men as today, when science has brought forth conveniences and comforts and luxuries of which our fathers did not dream, and made them available for the common man. In such a day it is easy for the world of the unseen to lose its meaning and power. And when the deeper needs of life are felt which mere things cannot satisfy, or the times of crisis come when our science and our machines are helpless, then faith in God and help from God are gone. And so we have today disillusionment, cynicism, and despair.

Nowhere is the loss of faith more apparent than when we turn to our national and international life. The responsible leaders of the nations are terribly afraid of war. They know what the late World War did and they realize that another might wipe out our Western civilization. But they cannot give up the old ways: the belief in force, the multiplication of armies on land and navies of sea and air, and national selfishness and greed. There is not faith enough to believe in a new way.

II. WHAT FAITH IS AND DOES

One reason why faith does not make more headway may be that both friends and enemies of religion have so often misunderstood it.⟩ Not many go as far as the small boy's definition, "Faith is believing what you know isn't so"; but many think of faith as something that is somehow against knowledge. For some it is "a leap in the dark." Knowledge, they think, deals only with what you can see; if you want to go beyond that, you simply shut your eyes and make the leap. Others think of faith as accepting a belief on the word of someone else—priest or preacher, Church or Bible. It is not hard to sympathize with those who reject faith if this is what it means. But faith is not unthinking submission to authority. The root of faith is inner conviction. Faith goes with freedom of spirit, not servitude. Jesus wanted faith; "Repent and believe in the good news," was his message. But he did not tell men that they must accept this doctrine or that because he said so. He said, "What think ye?" He showed them God and the truth of life, so that they might see and believe for themselves.

Nor does faith go against experience, rather it appeals to it just as science does; only it is the experience of a different kind of world. Natural science deals with the world of appearance, the world as it comes to us through our senses. We do not question the reality of this world or its importance; it is the world of our daily work, and our life depends upon it. But the world of the unseen is just as real and sure. We experience this unseen world just as truly as we do the seen, though in another way. Truth, love, loyalty, justice, the faith of a friend, the Spirit of God—I have never touched one of these with my hands, or seen it with my eyes, or weighed it in balances; but these are real, nevertheless. Religion says

they are the most real: that is why "we look not at
the things which are seen, but at the things which
are not seen; for the things which are seen are temporal; but the things which are not seen are eternal."
The difference between man and other animals is that
while both live in the world of the seen, man lives in
the world of the unseen as well; and there are found
the meaning of his life, the real ends for which he
lives, and the Power upon which he depends.

In the broadest sense faith is trust in a world that
is not seen and willingness to act upon this. In this
sense it belongs to all man's life, and is everywhere its
necessary foundation. That is true of the world of
business. The "hardheaded" business man must walk
by faith. Most of his dealings are with checks and
bills, bits of paper that have no value except as he
can trust the men or the government behind them.
When faith is gone, you have a crisis, a panic, a
depression. Science needs faith. "As for the strong
conviction that the cosmic order is rational," Thomas
Henry Huxley once wrote, "and the faith that,
throughout all duration, unbroken order has reigned
in the universe, I not only accept it, but I am dis-
posed to think it the most important of all truths."
This is, as Huxley saw, a matter of trust; science
assumes this order before it begins its work, and can
never prove it. It sees only the tiniest fraction of the
universe but believes that this order rules the vast
whole. It is so in the state. Autocracies rest upon
force and fear, but all other governments depend
upon faith, not only faith in men but faith in God, in
something just and true at the heart of things. That
was Lincoln's trust in the darkest days of the Civil

War: "Let us have faith that right makes might, and in that faith let us to the end dare to do our duty." Clearly, all the highest relations of men rest upon faith, a faith that is not irrational and not apart from experience, but that deals with the unseen and goes beyond what we can prove. The home rests upon it, all friendship, all love. As Romain Rolland says: "Love is a perpetual act of faith."

But the supreme importance of faith is found in religion. The unseen world, the world of order and truth, of beauty and love, of mercy and righteousness, breaks through everywhere in life. Religion gathers this all together and says: the world of the spirit is one, and its name is God.

> "They are but broken lights of thee,
>   And thou, O Lord, art more than they."

All these point to God and have their being in him. Therefore have faith in God. Believe that the true and good and beautiful are not only real, but the most real, that through all these God is speaking to you. And when you see all this at its highest, when you see the love and truth and righteousness that are in Jesus Christ, then trust this God that comes to you in him and surrender to him your life. Over against such a God the one thing needful is faith. Faith is the vision of the unseen, the trust in it, the surrender to it.

Faith thus rests upon experience, but transcends it; it sees what this experience means and trusts it, but goes beyond it. It demands not merely trust but obedience and loyalty and courage. It makes of life a high adventure instead of a timid surrender. San-

tayana calls us "to trust the soul's invincible surmise."
Josiah Royce, another great philosopher, described
faith as "the soul's insight or discovery of some reality that enables a man to stand anything that can
happen to him in the universe." Donald Hankey declared that it was "betting your life upon God."
Kirsopp Lake calls it "not belief in spite of evidence,
but life in scorn of consequence." It has been called
"the resolution to stand or fall by the noblest hypoth-
esis," and "man's Yes in trust and loyalty to the
highest that he knows." To which we may add the
word from Hebrews: "Now faith is assurance of
things hoped for, a conviction of things not seen."

III. The Battle of Faiths

We have been using the word "faith" for man's
attitude and act in believing; but we also speak of *a*
faith, that is, of the beliefs which man holds, his creed
or philosophy of life. It is such a faith that we wish
to consider in this volume. In the broadest sense of
the term everyone has a faith, something that he
believes in, something that he works for. The question is, What shall my faith be? There is today, as
there was when Christianity began, a battle of faiths,
each trying to win the allegiance of men. What is the
greatest rival of Christianity today? It is not, I
think, Hinduism, Buddhism, or Mohammedanism, or
any of the other world religions; it is secularism.

Secularism is a very common creed. The term
comes from a Latin word which meant originally generation, or age; it came to mean the passing age or
time, or the world. By secular we mean the finite
as against the Infinite, time as against the Eternal,

the visible as against the unseen, the world of things as against the world of spirit. Secularism is the creed that holds that there is nothing for man but this world and this age; there is no God above us, no life beyond, no authority except our own desire, no goods except material things. It stands squarely over against the central belief of religion, the faith in God, in a world that is unseen and enduring, that is near us and yet above us, and that gives our life its meaning, its hope, and its highest good.

This secularism has a double root. The first is doubt. Multitudes feel that they can no longer believe in an unseen world, that we must give up our faith in God, that our only knowledge is of things we see. Here are the "acids of modernity," of which Walter Lippmann writes in his *A Preface to Morals*. But there is another root and I think it is the deeper one. It is not so much the denial of another world as it is the belief in this world and the love of this world. That is paganism, and there is the real enemy of high religion. The paganism of today is not belief in idols or in "heathen gods." It is found just as much in London and New York as in Hong Kong and Calcutta. It has a triple creed: it believes in wealth as the highest good, in force and cunning as the supreme power, in self-interest as the one rule of life. It is manifest in the greed for wealth, the spirit of self-indulgence, the love of luxury, the measure of success in terms of money, and in an economic order in which the highest appeal is to a desire for individual advantage and the common method is ruthless competition.

Nationalism is one form which this modern paganism has taken and the cult of nationalism is the greatest rival of Christianity today. By nationalism is here meant not that love of country whose unselfish devotion goes with love of God and men, but that attitude which shuts out other peoples and puts the nation in the place of God. Externally, in regard to other peoples, it means a strictly selfish individualism. Within, it means totalitarianism, the claim of the political state to include all life and to dominate it all. Its true nature is best seen in Fascist Italy and Germany, where it is most fully developed, but in some measure it is present almost everywhere.

The three factors that enter into this modern supernationalism are commonly autocracy, militarism, and capitalism. (1) Autocracy may be vested in a political "leader," a military clique, or an economic group which controls the nation's industry and directs the government from behind the scenes. In an autocracy freedom of thought and speech and faith disappear. The final authority is not God or conscience or reason, but the state. Forms of religion remain, but they are made to serve the state. No appeal to conscience or God, for example, will save a man if the nation decides to go to war and kill. (2) Autocracy means militarism; the state depends upon force to compel its own people and to assert its will against other nations. Fascism means the rule of force. (3) In its present-day form Fascism means capitalism, that is, the control by the state or by a group within the state of the nation's material resources, and their use not for the people but for the state, or for the group in power. Competition remains, but it is between nations rather than individuals or groups.

Communism, as it is set up in Russia today, is like Fascism at certain points. It suppresses political freedom, it will not permit the Church to carry on any work of education, it is avowedly antireligious and secularistic, and it stands for the use of force, first in establishing the revolution, and, second, when needed, against other nations. It has sought to make a religion of Communism, demanding for it absolute faith and devotion, just as Fascism does. On the other hand, it has no desire for war, it seeks the social good of the masses instead of the few, it makes the state the instrument and not the end, and it substitutes economic co-operation for competitive war. It would seem, too, that its antireligious policy and its suppression of political freedom are not a necessary part of its system.

IV. A FAITH FOR TODAY

Here, then, are the reasons that make it important for us to inquire as to a faith for today. There is first the urgent need of some faith that will give meaning to life, that will supply confidence and courage, and that will bring guidance and authority. The alternatives for our day are literally faith or chaos. Secondly, there is the competition of the rival faiths of secularism and nationalism. Third, there are the questions and doubts which come from our new knowledge and which assail the old faith. Finally, there are the changes taking place in religious thought itself and the confusion as to what the Christian faith really is. Even before we begin this study one point seems clear: there is no higher form of religion offering itself than the Christian faith; no higher concept of God than that personal Spirit, just and merciful, whom we know through Jesus Christ; no loftier ideal of a way of life than that furnished by the spirit that was in Jesus.

He who would set forth a faith for today must face frankly two questions: Can we hold such a faith? And, Just what does such a faith mean in terms of belief and life? To answer these questions is not a simple matter. The short and easy way that men used to take was first to "prove" that the Christian religion was divine, and then simply to set forth the whole system of traditional ideas about God and the world, about man and salvation. Our plan must be different. We can no longer take complete systems on authority. We must see what this central conviction of the Christian faith is, this belief about God and life as we find it through Jesus. We must ask as to the right with which we hold such a faith. We must face all the facts that come to us from our world today, and take into account the highest insights which experience and reflection furnish. We must not be afraid of change; our concern is with the truth and our faith is in a living God, working in his world today and guiding men into the truth. And in the end we must realize that this God is more than what our minds can fully grasp or our ideas encompass, and that a God who was less than that could not command our faith and worship.

A Note for the Reader

Keeping in mind the use of this book by classes and discussion groups as well as by the individual reader, each chapter is furnished with questions and a brief book list. The questions are not intended for review purposes or to test the reader's knowledge but to aid in further study and group discussion.

The book lists are meant to be representative but not comprehensive. They reflect different standpoints, though no attempt is made to have all positions represented. A brief general list is first given containing works that will be of value for use throughout the volume. *The Encyclopedia of Religion and Ethics* and Hastings' *Dictionary of the Bible* are included because they are usually found in libraries. They will be referred to as E. R. E. and Hastings' D. B. The student should accustom himself to use these works and others of a general character in connection with the different chapters, looking up for himself the pertinent articles. One of the greatest helps to clear and sound thinking is the constant use of a good dictionary, and the habit of looking up all important terms and not letting a word pass whose meaning is not wholly clear.

The books listed have been selected with special reference to those who are beginning in this field rather than for the advanced student. In most cases the simpler and more popular treatments are put first. Some more advanced works are included for those who wish to make a more thorough study of a given question.

QUESTIONS FOR DISCUSSION

What are some of the common misconceptions about faith?

The relation of faith to knowledge; to authority; to experience.

The nature of faith as confidence; as courage; as loyalty (faithfulness) ; as adventure.

The place of faith in science, politics, business.

The place of faith in religion.

What faiths are the chief rivals of religion today?

SOME WORKS FOR GENERAL REFERENCE

James M. Hastings: *The Encyclopedia of Religion and Ethics*

James M. Hastings: *Dictionary of the Bible*

W. N. Clarke: *An Outline of Christian Theology*

E. D. Soper: *What May I Believe?*
A. Maude Royden: *I Believe in God*
Edwin Lewis: *A Manual of Christian Beliefs*
Georgia Harkness: *Conflicts in Religious Thought*
Wm. Adams Brown: *Christian Theology in Outline*
A. C. Knudson: *The Doctrine of God; The Doctrine of Redemption*
F. R. Tennant: *Philosophical Theology,* two vols.
W. R. Matthews: *Studies in Christian Philosophy*

For Further Reading

Harry Emerson Fosdick: *The Meaning of Faith*
Ernest F. Tittle: *Jesus After Nineteen Centuries*
Rufus M. Jones: *A Preface to Christian Faith in the New Age*
Walter M. Lippmann: *A Preface to Morals*
J. W. Nixon: *An Emerging Christian Faith*
D. M. Baillie: *Faith in God*
J. A. Leighton: *Religion and the Mind of Today* (especially Chap. XIX)
E. W. Lyman: *The Meaning and Truth of Religion,* Chap. IX.
Note also the books given in Chap. IV.

II

WHAT RELIGION IS AND DOES

NOT a few people today would rule religion out altogether. Religion, they say, is an outworn belief; the only real world is that which we see. Religion is a wrong dependence upon a higher power; the only help we have is in what we can do for ourselves. If we want health, let us turn to the physician; if money, to business; if knowledge, to science; if we have mental troubles, to the psychiatrist. Why, then, religion?

Now, the extraordinary fact is not the decay of religion but its persistence. The forms of religion change, its beliefs, its ways of worship, its organizations; but religion lives on. And the followers of religion include the highest as well as the humblest, the lands of light and leading as well as backward races. The publishers will tell you that the field of religion ranks with the highest in number of books produced and sold. In periods of panic or depression, there are fewer closed churches than bank failures. Religions change, religion persists. The very change suggests that we have in religion not a dead institution but something living and growing, that there is something in the very nature of reality, of man and his world, from which religion springs. What, then, are the roots of religion?

THE ROOTS OF RELIGION

1. Its first root is in man. That is why religion

lasts. If it were a mere invention of priests, as some have said, or a mistaken theory about the world and life, or something incidental and insignificant, it would have disappeared long since from the enlightened nations, if not from the whole world. It lives on because there is something deep and abiding in human life to which religion answers. Most human life is lived in two dimensions, a man's self and his world, the world including both things and men. Religion is life in three dimensions: a man's self, his world, and God. But the important point is not that we add belief in God to the other two, but, rather, that the third dimension changes a man's whole world. Religion can rightly say: "Behold, I make all things new." In religion we have not simply God but a new and deeper meaning for man's self and his whole world.

Religion meets three basic needs of humanity. First, we want to know not simply facts, such as science brings, but the meaning of facts, whether our life has any end beyond eating and drinking, sleeping and waking through our few years, and then turning again to the dust from which we came. What does life signify? Does our life fit in to something high and enduring? Second, we want to be. We want life, and life is more than existence or pleasure. Man is the one creature that lives in two worlds, the world that is and that which is to be. He belongs to this higher world. In it lie all the beauty and truth and goodness and love which he has not yet realized in his life. He knows that his real life lies somewhere there ahead. He sees the highest and he cannot be satisfied except as he seeks

it. Third, we want help. We know only too well
the evil within us, the lower that defeats the higher,
the evil that fights against the good. We are divided
within, and division means defeat. We are frag-
ments; by ourselves we are nothing, and we want to
be complete. We seek for something higher to which
to give ourselves, something greater in which we can
find life and strength.

This is why religion lives. Men may reject this
answer or that given in the name of religion, but they
will always be interested in these questions. A man's
religion is his answer to these needs. Every man,
so far as he rises above the level of the brute, must
seek an answer to these problems which are the final
problems of life. Other interests come and go;
religion remains the supreme concern of man just
because he is man.

2. The real root of religion is not man but God,
the God who has made man with such needs and
who is the answer to the needs that he has made.
God comes first. Religion is not an invention but a
response; it is man's answer to the unseen world.
As sight is the answer to the world of light, hearing
to the world of sound, reason to the order of the
universe, and love to other spirits like our own, so
religion is the answer to that third dimension of the
universe, the Eternal that is infinitely above us but
at the same time everywhere reaches down into our
finite world and gives it meaning. The tides of this
vast world of the unseen beat upon these lives of
ours. Slowly man becomes aware of God, more
slowly still he learns what God is. Some have found
him through truth, more through love, some in the

sense of awe before a strange holiness and majesty like that of the solemn heavens at night, some in the voice of conscience that holds before us the lofty and unbending claim of what is right and good. Religion is not our imagining. It is not wish-thinking. God is not something that we have compounded of our wishes and fears, and then projected into the heavens. The unseen world is there. Religion is our dim surmise of something vaster than all our thinking, something that has searched us and known us, that has beset us behind and before and laid its hand upon us. There will always be religion just because God is, because there is an Eternal that is above all change, a Holiness that is above our sin and folly, a Purpose that is waiting to give meaning to our lives, a Love that will not let us go.

II. What Religion Is and Does

Now we begin to see what religion is. There are endless definitions of religion. Not many of them are false; their fault is that they are only part of the truth. Religion is so great that we are apt to see only one aspect of it. For one man religion means correct belief; for another simply being good and doing good; for a third it is a mystical sense of awe and wonder, the stirring of heart in the presence of the Infinite. It is all these, and more. When man meets the Highest and bows before it, that is religion: "the deepest response of the self to the highest that we know." Here are at least two things involved: first, we find that Being before whose holiness we bow, in whose goodness we trust, upon whose power we feel that our life depends; second, we give ourselves to this Being in trust and obedience. In a word, religion means to find God, to see all things in his light, to do all by his strength and according to his will. There is thus a faith that engages the mind, a trust that involves the heart, an obedience that commands the will.

What, then, does religion do for man? What does it give us that we do not already have in business and pleasure, in science and art, in literature and learning? Now, religion does not exclude any of these, but these are all parts; religion is concerned with the whole and the highest. The task of religion is to lead man into the presence of the Most High and thus to show him the meaning of the whole and the way of life. We can put the gift of religion to man in three words: insight, right relations, life.

1. Religion brings insight. Sight is a good thing; it shows us this and that of which our world is made. But the trouble is that we see parts and not the whole, the surface and not the heart of things. Religion bids us look at the whole and ask what all this means, this world and this life of ours. To sight it adds insight and understanding. It bids us see one power, one purpose, one Spirit of goodness that is back of all things. It shows us God; and when we have found him, then everything else falls into place. Life is no longer empty and futile; our own life, even the humblest, gains a high meaning by being joined to the purpose of God.

2. Religion brings right relations. Adjustment, integration, right relation are words constantly emphasized today, and with right, for their absence is the source of the world's sin and suffering and

unhappiness. We are divided within; we are not at peace even with ourselves. We are out of harmony with our fellows—man and man, nation and nation. We are not in right relation even with the world of things; in our greed and lust and self-indulgence we let that harm us which God placed here for our service. And, through ignorance and indifference and disobedience, we are out of right relation with God. Here, then, is the function of religion, first to bring us into fellowship with God, then through this fellowship to give us the guidance and motive and power for a new life, and so to set us into right relations with our fellows and our world. Religion means unity.

3. Religion brings life. For life comes always and only through right relations. When those are established, then the misunderstandings and antagonisms, the hatreds and fears, the weakness and failure, are overcome, and the way is opened to confidence and peace and strength.

This, then, is what religion does: It bids men see life whole; it shows man the world that is not seen; it reveals the rich and thrilling possibilities of life; it brings men into the presence of the Most High; it bids men bow in worship and rise with new confidence and high purpose; it sets man right with God and his world so that he may come to fullness of life for himself and richness of life in service.

And now we can see why religion is not only central in life but why it must be supreme. "The utmost for the highest" is the word that marks religion. Unless it brings the highest and demands the utmost it is not real religion.

"Religion's all or nothing; it's no mere smile
O' contentment, sigh of aspiration, sir—
No quality of the finelier-tempered clay
Like its whiteness or its lightness; rather, stuff
O' the very stuff; life of life, and self of self."

III. The Marks of Religion

What now are the marks of a truly religious man?
What will be his inner spirit and attitude? It is
interesting to see where the great teachers have
found it. Not in pious phrases ("Not every one that
saith Lord, Lord"), not in free religious utterance
("The tongues of men and of angels"), not in strict
observance of ritual and rule ("I fast twice a week,
I give tithes of all that I get"), nor in correct opinion
("The devils believe and tremble"). Rather, it has
been in certain simple, though deep-reaching elements. We may begin with one of the great prophets,
Micah, who spoke centuries before Socrates and
Plato, and even before Buddha and Confucius.
Lincoln once said that his words might well be put
upon the walls of every church and temple: "What
doth the Lord require of thee, but to do justly, and
to love mercy, and to walk humbly with thy God?"
Paul puts it in just four words: "faith working
through love," and then more concretely and fully
in his great chapter on love, ending with the triad,
faith, hope, and love. Jesus sums it up in his double
command, taken from the Old Testament, to love God
with heart and mind and soul and strength, and our
neighbor as ourselves. We shall get Jesus' idea even
more clearly if we study first the beatitudes, then
the Lord's Prayer.

In all this we see religion not as word or deed or

belief or emotion, but as inner spirit and attitude. (1) There is the attitude of the religious man as he looks up. He is the man who sees the invisible, and lives in its presence and by its power. The intangibles of life count with him: beauty, truth, justice, mercy. Above all, he has the sense of God, and toward God the spirit of reverence, awe, and adoration. (2) There is an attitude with which he looks out upon men and the world. He not only sees the unseen but lives by it. Therefore he owns the world and is not owned by it, whether by lust or fear. For his fellow men he has not only pity but reverence; he sees them, however low in the scale, as those who belong to God and are made for him. And beyond the world that is, with its ignorance and evil and unhappiness, he sees the world that God is shaping, the realm of peace and justice, of truth and mercy, that is yet to be. (3) There is a religious attitude in man's inner self: humility, a sense of dependence, a realization of individual sin and shortcoming; but also high aspiration, a spirit of adventure, a courageous daring which belongs to one who has seen and believed and now goes forward undismayed at what comes because the event is with God.

QUESTIONS FOR DISCUSSION

Why does religion persist when its empirical forms are so commonly imperfect in ideas and practices?

What are the main elements that go to make up a man's religion?

What should religion do for a man?

What should religion do for society?

Who is the (ideally) religious man?

What are the chief hindrances to religion within the individual life?

What conditions or influences in society are most dangerous to religion?

FOR FURTHER READING

The following works should be used in connection with later chapters as well:

J. B. Pratt: *The Religious Consciousness*

William James: *The Varieties of Religious Experience*

E. W. Lyman: *The Meaning and Truth of Religion*

D. M. Edwards: *A Philosophy of Religion*

E. S. Brightman: *A Philosophy of Ideals*

G. T. W. Patrick: *An Introduction to Philosophy*

W. K. Wright: *A Student's Philosophy of Religion*

R. H. Thouless: *Introduction to the Psychology of Religion*

H. T. Houf: *What Religion Is and Does*

III

WHAT IS THE CHRISTIAN RELIGION?

I. Christianity in History

ASK what Christianity is and we get a score of answers, each differing from the others. It will help us if, first of all, we consider Christianity as a historical movement. In so doing we shall discover three stages, the first that of preparation marked especially by a People; the second, its central creative point as marked by a Person; the third, its continuing life as represented by a Fellowship.

1. To understand Christianity we must begin with the People, the Hebrews. Many other influences entered into the forming of the new religion, but this has a unique place. The Jews were never a great nation. Their land was small; it could have been dropped down within the borders of any one of a score of states in the United States. They had no great power; almost their whole history can be told in terms of those ancient empires to which they were in turn subjected: Egypt, Assyria, Babylonia, Macedonia, Syria, Rome. They had no art or philosophy of their own, and no great men of letters. But they had something more significant: they had prophets, seers, saints, men with deep insight and a hunger for God. Long centuries have passed. The whole shape of life has been changed. But when we ask the great questions that concern man, the questions about righteousness and mercy and God, then these prophets are still

our teachers, their prayers and hymns are still our inspiration and help. The Old Testament is the background and basis of Christianity. It was the Bible and hymnal and prayer book of the primitive Church. There were, of course, "Hebrew old clothes" that needed to be gotten rid of. The Old Testament is not all on one level; Jesus selected and corrected in his use of it, but he himself was nurtured in the faith of the prophets and the piety of the psalms. You cannot understand the New Testament without the Old.

2. The second stage and central point of this history is marked by a Person, Jesus. What went before had its consummation in him; all who came after look to him as Lord. Many influences bore upon growing Christianity: the mystery religions with their passionate desire for redemption from this world and their belief in the power of sacramental rites, Greek philosophy whose ideas the early theologians used, Rome with its stress on rule and organization, and the varied social and economic conditions of that age. But Christ was the creative source. It was round him that the first disciples gathered. He gave them their faith and led them into fellowship with God. He gave them their hope for the future and his spirit was their rule of life. And he has remained center and source and inspiration through the ages, not as a memory of the past but as a living presence.

3. The third stage is that of the Fellowship which we call the Church. In the strict sense, historical Christianity began only when Jesus left and the Church arose. We must be careful lest the word "Church" give us a wrong picture; for Church suggests an institution, forms of organization, central

authority, clerical orders, creeds, and ritual. But Christianity did not begin that way. It was first a fellowship, rather loosely united so far as outward bonds were concerned, but consciously one through the ties of the spirit, one in a common faith, love, and loyalty, one in the deep sense of a divine Presence. We watch this fellowship spread through the Roman world. It creates its own sacred writings, the New Testament, and sets them beside the Old Testament to form one sacred book. It defines its faith and formulates creeds. From the beginning, as the New Testament makes plain, there are different groups and varying points of view. There is no prescribed creed or organization. It was a vigorous life that could not be kept in rigid molds or held to one pattern. The fellowship gradually divided into separate "churches," often with bitter conflicts. Leaders tried to establish authoritative forms of organization and belief which should remain unchanged; but even apart from its divisions, the Church itself never remained exactly the same in any two generations.

II. WHAT IS THE ESSENCE OF CHRISTIANITY?

It was inevitable that among these Christians the question should arise as to the essence of Christianity. No Christian body ever looked at this history as merely a human affair. It was history but more than history; it was a revelation of God and a way of salvation. So men asked: Just what is the divine element in this religion? Or, put in another way, What is the essence of Christianity? Of the many answers given we may select a half dozen that are representative.

(1) Christianity is the Church, says Roman Catholicism, this specific visible organization with the Pope of Rome at the head. That was what Christ established to represent him upon earth. To this institution he committed the divine and infallible threefold power which he possessed, that is, the power of teaching, of rule, and of salvation. The Church is the Christian religion. (2) The ancient Greek Orthodox faith likewise holds much the same view, but its conception of the Church is more mystical and less legalistic. Sometimes it has put supreme emphasis on the creeds—hence the name "Orthodox." But more vital and significant is the thought as set forth by certain of its leaders today of the Church as a living organism, the body of Christ, animated by the divine life and mediating that life to men through the sacraments. (3) The Bible is Christianity, some Protestants have said; at least, here is its divine and absolute element and men have simply to believe what it teaches and do what it says. (4) Some, accepting this conception of the Bible, have found the essence of Christianity in a sum of teachings which God has revealed through the Bible, in certain doctrines which are the absolute and unchanging "fundamentals of the faith." (5) Christianity is the religion of the spirit, others have said, and especially the Quakers. Not organization or doctrine or ritual is essential, but the Spirit which God gives to men for strength and guidance, and a certain inner quality of spirit which is the true religion in man. (6) For still others the mystical seems vague and creed and ritual incidental, or even an obstacle; for them the essential element in Christianity, as in all religion, is practical,

and the Church is to be "the union of those that love in the service of those that need."

III. Two Ways of Looking at Christianity

It is not likely that Christian men will ever agree as to just what is the divine essence in Christianity. The question is whether men have not been approaching the whole matter from the wrong standpoint. There is a deeper problem involved here, and that is how we are to think of God in his relation to the world. Christianity, all these agree, is something divine; but how does the divine enter the world? There are two ways of answering this question, and they determine largely the answer to the other query as to what Christianity is.

1. The first way we may call, for convenience, dualism and institutionalism. It is dualistic in its idea of God's relation to the world. It emphasizes strongly the transcendence of God and the idea of God as the "wholly other." God stands over against his world and works directly and from without. What he does is in no way dependent upon man, nor is it conditioned by the slow movement of history. It is God's deed and God's alone, and therefore it is absolute and perfect.

From this dualism there comes what we may call the "institutional" idea of Christianity. It recognizes, of course, the human and historical side of Christianity, and so the element of imperfection and change. But if Christianity is divine, then, it is assumed, there must be something in it that is perfect and unchangeable, something which God himself has instituted, which he has given directly to man. The traditional theology of both Catholics and Protestants agreed at this point. They differed in their ideas of what this was that God had given to men. The "Catholic" groups found it in the Church, the Protestants in the Bible or some sum of doctrines. Both sought for something objective, definite, tangible. Both felt that it must be infallible and unchanging because it was strictly supernatural, coming direct from God.

But to this position, in whatever form it is held, three objections must be raised, and these become more and more clear as men face the problem with open minds.

(1) History nowhere shows us any such infallible and unchanging element which we can separate out of the historic movement of Christianity. What we see is a new and powerful spiritual life, a profound conviction that God had come in Jesus Christ, and a faith and love which bound men together in a great fellowship. Now, life always needs a body through which to function; that is true of the group life as it is of the individual. The Christian fellowship had to have organization and leadership; it had to have forms of worship, ritual, and sacraments; out of its life there grew certain writings, like the Gospels and the letters of Paul, and these were kept as serving a permanent need; and from the beginning men sought to interpret to themselves and others what this life and faith meant, and so there were confessions, theologies, and creeds. These four factors form the institutional side of Christianity, or, to use a better figure, the body shaped by the spirit and expressing its life. Because this was something definite, because

men found God through fellowship and Scriptures and worship and teaching, it was natural that these should be called divine; and because men thought of them as divine, they naturally conceived them in time as being infallible. But the plain facts are to the contrary. The creeds of the Church are man's attempt to set forth the truth of his faith; they are fallible and changing. The Bible is human as well as divine; it did not drop complete and perfect from the skies, but came forth out of man's life. The New Testament gives no basis for the "Catholic" idea of the Church as a supernaturally established institution, with legally prescribed form of organization, to whose hierarchy all was committed; history shows, rather, that in every aspect there was a gradual development, with a full share of human fallibility in teaching and rule.

(2) There is a misconception here as to how God works in the world. It was very simple and natural that men should think of God as above the earth, external to it, moving upon it by direct and irresistible action; that they should suppose that if Christianity were divine, we should be able to put our finger upon something which God himself had wrought, which he had handed down to men, and which as such was infallible, whether Bible, creed, or Church. But in actual fact, God does not work that way. Wherever we find him, in the Bible, in the Church, in the life of men today, he works in and through human life and experience.

(3) The emphasis on the "institutional" brings certain dangers to religion. The heart of religion is spiritual and ethical: an inner attitude of reverence, faith, and devotion, and a way of life; the institu-

tional tends to turn the attention to something that is at least relatively external: submission to authority, acceptance of beliefs, and performance of ritual. Religion means something living and therefore growing and advancing, whether you think of the living God at work in the world or of the divine life in man; institutionalism tends to make religion static, to let it petrify in fixed ideas and forms, or stagnate in a formal routine of words and action. So men come at last to care more for the institution than the life, to overlook real religion while acting as zealous "defenders of the faith," of Bible and creed and Church, and in doing this to reveal the closed mind and the narrow, intolerant, and even vindictive spirit.

2. There is a second way of conceiving God's relation to the world. He is still the transcendent God, more than the world; but he is not apart from the world, not set over against it or external to it. Whether he works to reveal himself, to guide men into the truth, or to give men life, it is not through something that he hands over: a creed, a book, or an organization. It is, rather, as indwelling Spirit, as a divine life working in history and human experience. Christianity is the religion of the living God, but he is a God who works patiently, slowly, from within, not in a "direct action" that is external, irresistible, and absolute.

From all this there follows the spiritual, or vital-historical, conception of Christianity. It has its dangers also, the danger that Christianity shall become vague and uncertain, that we shall lose the divine in emphasizing the historical and human, that all shall become relative and men shall never be sure of God.

self, so far as we gain it, is not transcended. There is an eternal world of beauty and truth and goodness; man does not create it, he discovers it, and so far as he really discovers it, it abides. Greek sculpture, the paintings of the masters, the work of Bach and Mozart and Beethoven will never be left behind. So there are insights in religion which can never alter. Twenty-seven centuries ago the Hebrew prophets saw that religion meant, not sacrifices to placate God or gifts to win his favor, but humble trust, simple obedience, and justice and mercy shown to man. No coming years will ever make obsolete the word of Micah, already quoted, "What doth the Lord require of thee, but to do justly, and to love mercy, and to walk humbly with thy God?"

We have many things yet to learn, and a still longer road to travel in translating truth into life; but the word of God to man which has come in Jesus Christ so far from being transcended still moves far in advance of human progress. The God whom he made known is still the God of our faith—no higher vision has been given to us. We have endless problems to solve in our individual and social life, but he has showed us the kind of men that we should be and the spirit that should govern our life together.

V. THE RELIGION OF REDEMPTIVE GOOD WILL

We have found the unique character of the Christian religion, its divine element, not in the letter of the Bible, or in a sum of doctrine, or in any given institution, but in the spirit that was in Christ seen as the revelation of what God is, of what man is to be, and of the way of man's salvation. Scholars tell us that we cannot be absolutely certain that Jesus' words have been correctly reported to us in any given passage, or that we have exactly or in order the details of his life story; yet clearly, definitely, and with convincing reality his spirit stands forth from the pages of the Gospels. But just what is that spirit? No one word can express it, nor, indeed, all our words. The best single word is love, if only that word had not been so much sentimentalized and de-moralized in common use. Without giving up that great word, let us call it the spirit of holy and redemptive good will: holy because it is something transcendent, divine, and righteous; good will because it seeks nobly and highly as well as unselfishly the supreme good of its object; redemptive because there is in it not simply a high goal but a power to transform. Or, more briefly, we might call Christianity the religion of creative good will. The meaning of this is clear if we consider this in relation to the three great life questions with which religion deals: the God in whom we trust, the life that we must lead, the power on which we depend for help.

1. Through Christ we learn, and dare to believe, that God is redemptive good will. The Power that is back of this universe of ours is holiness and righteousness; but it is more. It is love that is constantly seeking to win men from evil, to call them into its own life. What Jesus was and did in his life of love and sacrifice, that we believe God was and is and is now doing.

2. This is the life that men must lead. It is not the only word to use but it is the central word. Paul said this in his great chapter on love, 1 Corinthians

13. Jesus declared, "Ye therefore shall be perfect, as your heavenly Father is perfect"; and this word follows a matchless passage in which he describes the love of God that draws no lines, and that no disobedience or ingratitude of men can change. The rule of life for the Christian religion is nothing less than the Spirit of God as seen in Christ.

3. And good will is the way of salvation. Here is the only power that can save us. That is the "good news," the gospel, which Christianity has declared from the beginning. God does not save men by commandment or might or wisdom, but by his forgiving love that wins them, and by that same love as a transforming force in their hearts. What we have been slower to learn is that this good will, and this alone, as practiced in human relations between man and man, between nation and nation, can heal the world's wounds and save it from disaster. Christianity stands inflexibly for that way as against all national pride and international rivalry, against all militarism and imperialism, against all the ways of selfishness and force. Here is the test of a Christian faith: to surrender our own life in unfaltering trust and obedience to the God of saving good will, and then, with equal courage and confidence, renouncing force and selfishness and guile, to build the individual life and our social order upon this same principle.

VI. THE RELIGION OF THE SPIRIT

The Christian religion as seen in the New Testament reveals two striking features which makes it deserve the name of the religion of the spirit.

1. The emphasis of the New Testament is upon the inner spirit in religion. Jesus goes back of laws and forms and institutions and opinions. Humility, reverence, faith, obedience, unconquerable good will— these determine whether men are children of their Father. If any man have not the spirit of Christ, Paul says, he is none of his, but if he have this spirit, which is God's Spirit, then he has life and joy and peace, then he can say, "Abba, Father." This does not deny the place of form and organization in religion. Christianity means a fellowship, it means work in the world; and so forms of worship, confessions of faith, organized activity, and leadership are needed. But all this is secondary. It is here to express and advance the life of the spirit, as instrument and not as end.

2. The New Testament shows us the religion of the Spirit in a second sense; this higher spirit in man which it demands is the creation of the Spirit of God. New Testament religion is an ellipse drawn about two foci, Christ and the Spirit. In Christ God has come to man; in the Spirit God works creatively in men. But the two foci sometimes move so close together, especially in Paul, that it looks like a circle with one center: Christ is present with men as Spirit, and the Spirit is that of Christ. So Paul says flatly: "Now the Lord [Christ] is the Spirit." But the important fact is this: God is not distant power but living Presence; religion is no mere human effort, it is God's gift. And so Christianity appears as a religion of inspiration and power, as a gift and not a mere task, as a life given to men as well as one to be lived.

VII. Permanence and Advance

From this there have followed two facts of great-est importance for the movement of Christianity through the centuries, facts which seem to form a paradox: Christianity has been a religion of freedom and change and advance; Christianity has main-tained its identity in all the centuries and has not lost its true self.

1. Christianity has been a religion of freedom and advance because it is a religion of the spirit and not one of hard and fixed institution and form. Our God is the God of the spirit, working here and now, the God of life that ever moves on, the God at work ever achieving anew, the God of truth to whom all truth belongs. And he guides us into new life and truth by his Spirit. We do not live in the past. If there is truth from science, truth found in other faiths, we take it, for it all belongs to the God of truth. The faith we have through Christ is not an enclosure to which we retreat for safety and rest; rather, it is an open highway along which we adven-ture, knowing that the living God leads the way.

2. In a very true sense, however, Christianity has remained the same. We have not gone beyond Christ, not gone off on another way; we have fol-lowed him. We do not stop with Christ but he gives us the line of advance. Our organization, our theol-ogies, our rules, our life—none of these has been per-fect or final. But one thing has been certain and has not changed: it is the faith that in Jesus Christ there is revealed to us what God is and what man must be. All our life has confirmed this. The ages

have shown us no higher vision of God, no truer way of life. Still we turn to Christ and say:

> "We own thy sway, we hear thy call,
> We test our lives by thine."

Let us sum up what Christianity is in three different forms of statement which yet are one. (1) Historically, Christianity is that ongoing and ever-renewed fellowship that had its origin in Jesus Christ, and that finds in him its continuing inspiration and guidance. (2) Essentially, Christianity is the religion of redemptive good will: it believes in the God of good will, in the life of good will for men, and in the final triumph of the spirit of good will on earth. (3) In one word, Christianity is Christ, the Christ through whom we know what God is and what man is to be.

QUESTIONS FOR DISCUSSION

The tendency to institutionalism (ecclesiasticism) in religion and the defects and dangers of this type of Christianity.

Individualistic, subjective, and liberalistic trends, and their dangers.

What do you consider the primary elements which go to make up the Christian religion?

What should be our attitude toward non-Christian faiths? What should be the grounds, the spirit, and the method of Christian work in non-Christian lands?

Can we have a religion which is final and yet leaves room for progress in thought and life?

FOR FURTHER READING

E. R. E.: Articles, "Jesus Christ," "Christianity"
Edwyn Bevan: *Christianity*
H. R. Mackintosh: *The Originality of the Christian Message*

E. Stanley Jones: *The Christ of the Indian Road*
Oscar Buck: *Christianity Tested*
Edwin Lewis: *A Christian Manifesto*
H. F. Rall and S. S. Cohon: *Christianity and Judaism Compare Notes*
Karl Adam: *The Spirit of Catholicism*
Adolf Harnack: *What Is Christianity?*
John Baillie: *The Place of Jesus Christ in Modern Christianity*
T. R. Glover: *The Jesus of History; Jesus in the Experience of Men*
C. E. Raven: *Jesus and the Gospel of Love*
D. Elton Trueblood: *The Essence of Spiritual Religion*
H. T. Andrews and others: *The Lord of Life*
W. P. Paterson: *The Rule of Faith*
Nicholas Arseniev: *We Beheld His Glory*

IV

FAITH IN GOD

THERE are some who are more sure of God than of life itself; God, indeed, is their life. But most of us have questions to meet about faith in God, questions rising in our own minds or brought by others. The questions usually move around two points: Can we prove the being of God? If we cannot prove, what right have we to believe?

I. THE GROUNDS FOR BELIEF IN GOD

Let it be said at once, you cannot prove the being of God any more than you can "prove" by logic that love and truth and right are real, or that man is more than a temporary arrangement of physical particles. The things that count most in life are not proved, they are experienced. No man ever believed in God because God was demonstrated. There are, however, grounds which appeal to the reason. They rest back upon our experience and suggest that such experience points to belief in God and is most reasonably explained by the idea of God. We will turn in order to the main fields in which we have our experience and see why it is that men believe in God.

1. The most common reason why people believe in God is because those round about them do so; we are brought up in this belief. Many would say that this was no ground at all, that we ought to reject tradition and authority as unworthy of free and thinking

men, that though childhood begins by taking its ideas from others, we must not remain children. The emphasis on individual experience and inner conviction is in the spirit of Protestantism and of all high religion, yet there are some facts here that must not be overlooked. (1) The experience of any one man is limited; we should be poor, indeed, not only in religion but everywhere else, if we were confined to what we could discover for ourselves. But there are experiences of the group and the race in which we can share discoveries in the world of the spirit which the ages have made and tested. We must not take them blindly and unthinkingly; we must weigh and choose and try out. But we have the right to give great weight to these when we determine the faith by which we shall live. (2) Our capacities and abilities are limited. That is why we accept gladly the discoveries and creations of the geniuses in science and art and letters. Just so there have been great souls in religion, the seers and prophets and saints of the ages, more quick to see, more sensitive to the voice of God, more ready to receive his life. The greatest spirits of our race through long ages have believed in God. It is right that we learn from their insights and find in their faith a ground for our faith.

2. The world of nature points toward God. True, we no longer argue from the world to God as men could argue from a watch to a watchmaker. This universe has come to be through long ages of change by the operation of forces working within it, not by some divine Carpenter working from outside. But the question still remains: What is the nature of

this Force that is working in this world? Look at some of the characteristics of our universe. (1) It is a world of order throughout, not haphazard, or of one order here and another in the distant stars. (2) It is a world of beauty. Sir J. Arthur Thomson, in his *System of Animate Nature,* has pointed out that except for the abnormal and for the occasional parasitic creature, beauty is a characteristic of every form of life. The same beauty appears in inanimate being: in star and crystal and snowflake. (3) It is a world of development, moving slowly but steadily from the lowest forms to the highest: matter, life, mind, spirit. You may try to account for this in one of three ways. (1) Materialism, or pure naturalism, declares that only the physical is real, and that all this beauty and order and goodness have come by mere chance working blindly through endless change; that the mind of an Aristotle, the dramas of Shakespeare, the spirit of Francis of Assisi, and the drifting desert sands are all and equally nothing but chance collocations of particles of matter. But if people think that the medieval saints were credulous, what shall we say of this idea, that matter produces spirit, blindness brings forth sight, that order comes out of anarchy, something out of nothing! As Thomas H. Huxley once put it: "Is the universe a mud pie made by two blind children, Nature and Force?" One might as well suppose, to borrow an old figure, that a thousand children throwing letter blocks on the floor for a thousand years might someday produce Macbeth or King Lear, or a thousand monkeys at a thousand pianos if they pounded long enough might bring forth a Beethoven Symphony.

(2) A second theory, more popular today, thinks of the universe in terms not of separate particles but of a kind of organism in which there is working a Life Force, a Creative Energy, or some kind of organizing Principle that slowly brings things into right relations and so gradually produces order and higher forms of being. This is a real advance. There is plainly some such creative co-ordination going on in the process of evolution. But is it blind or purposive, is it force or mind? Can the lower bring forth the higher, the stream rise above its source? (3) There remains the belief that the world is best understood as the work of a Spirit that is conscious, rational, purposive, and good. Such a Being would account for both the order within which all change takes place, and for the progress that is made within that order which at last brings forth the highest fruits of the spirit.

3. The world of moral experience, of the experience of values, requires faith in God. Let us make this broad enough to include all the ideals and values of life, all that is true and beautiful and good. A man can, of course, reject all spiritual values. He may believe only in things that he sees, may live only for wealth that he can own or for physical pleasure, and recognize no authority except his own selfish will. It is a question whether even such men, deep down in their hearts, really escape moral reality and its authority. Certainly, most of us do not, and do not wish to. It is these ideals and values that lift us above the common brute and give meaning to our life. Many a man in his hour of doubt, when faith in God has seemed impossible, has said to himself,

"There is such a thing as truth and love and justice and honor, and I will follow these." What does this moral experience imply? We do not make these ideals, we discover them. When we find them, they speak to us with authority and we recognize their right to command. When we obey them, our lives fall into right relations with other lives and with our world, and we gain strength, satisfaction, and peace. When we disobey them, there is discord without, disintegration within, weakness, fear, failure, destruction. And that applies to nations as it does to individuals, especially if we follow history through the long ages.

What does all this mean? Which way do these insights and experiences point? Plainly, the logic of all this suggests that these ideals and values of the spirit are not accidents or incidents or merely human invention; they belong to the essential nature of our universe, the very warp and woof of things. Our discovery of the moral universe may be slow, our insights and ideals may change, just as our understanding of the physical world through the ages has been almost incredibly slow. But the world of the right and good and true is there waiting for us as nature waits for the scientist; and it is something fundamental and enduring, something real and ultimate. But that means that the Being that is back of all appearing, and that is working in all change, is moral being; and moral being means personal being, and moral personal being means God. To believe in God means to believe that the final being and power in this world is not things or brute force, but a personal Spirit that is good. For these ideals and values cannot live as mere abstractions. Beauty exists only for minds that see and appreciate. Love and righteousness are mere abstractions except as they live in beings that can love and follow what is just and true. The world of moral experience points to God and depends on him. And in history, when men have ceased to believe in God the world of moral ideals has lost its reality for man and its authority for his life; and then human society moves on to collapse.

4. Besides society and nature and morals, there is a fourth world of experience, the religious. Religion really takes in all life as its sphere, but we use it here in the narrower sense as meaning man's immediate awareness of something high and holy, before which he bows in reverence, upon which he knows that he depends.

— The final ground for religious faith is found within religion, not outside of it. It is with religion just as it is with the other fundamental beliefs of life; you do not begin with an idea which you try to prove, you begin with an experience which you then try to understand. The ideas come out of the experience and are our effort to interpret it.) Something "out there" comes to me and acts upon me; I react, respond to it. There begins thus a life of active intercourse. I try to understand what comes to me in this way, to express it in ideas and words. So I am convinced that the world of things is real, though the scientist tells me I do not know it as it is. That is why my friend is real to me. I have never seen him, the man himself, his personal spirit; I have only seen color and form, heard sounds which I called his

voice, felt his body. I cannot prove that there is a
personal spirit there like myself. And yet there is
this intercourse, this action, reaction, response; and I
know him.

That is the real reason why men believe in God.
The persistence of religion is one of the most extraordinary facts in human history. Central to it is the
belief in a spiritual world, in forces that are not seen
but are real, in God. The ideas have varied greatly.
Experience and reflection have led men to reject this
or the other as imperfect or false, but the belief has
remained. It is hard to explain that on any other
ground than that which religion itself assigns: Something There has spoken to us, has come into our life;
and we name it God. You may call this religious
insight or mysticism or the sense of the Holy, but no
definition can contain it. It comes in the feelings of
reverence and awe, in the sense of dependence, in the
moral experience where we hear a word that commands with authority, in the mind's vision of a world
of unity and order and meaning that transcends the
individual and the moment, and, finally, in the
strength and enrichment of life that comes when
following these insights and demands. We know we
are in actual intercourse with the world of the spirit,
just as in everyday life we know when we deal with
the world of things or men. It is this experience,
repeated in all ages, available to all who will meet
the necessary conditions, that explains the persistence of belief in God and so of religion.

II. The Right to Believe

And now we must meet a final question. What right

have we to believe? We have considered the grounds for belief in God as brought by history, by nature, and by our experience in the moral and religious realms. In the end, however, it remains true: you cannot point God out so that men will see him with their eyes, or prove him logically so that men will have to accept him. No man can have God except by an act of faith. From the very nature of the case we cannot prove the Infinite by the finite, or the unseen by the seen. Every one of the "grounds" that we considered implied an act of trust in something that could not be demonstrated. And so we are challenged as to the right to believe. Since religion deals with the supreme issues and interests of human life, ought we not to wait till we have absolute proof? For the thoughtful and earnest man the answer, I think, must be No.

1. If our first business in life were logic, then our first concern would be proof; but our first business is living, and that demands faith. In Bergson's words: "Speculation is a luxury, while life is a necessity"; so we have the right to that which is necessary to the business of living. The necessity of faith appears in every activity of life. There is little that we can demonstrate; there is much upon which we must and do act. And the most important matters are those least capable of demonstration to the senses or by logic. Everywhere we deal with the invisible, with the imponderables, with values that are appreciated rather than things that are weighed and measured; and we are compelled to trust. The scientist himself has to do that: he trusts his senses, his reason, the reason of his fellow workers, and, above all, the pres-

ence of a universal and trustworthy natural order which confessedly he can never prove. He cannot even begin his work without such faith. So the statesman must have faith in his own people and in other nations; when that breaks down, there is nothing left but force and mutual destruction. So the business man trusts others; almost all his business is done with bits of paper—paper money, checks, notes, bonds, items of credit and debit in account—worthless in themselves, of value only as there is faith in what he cannot see. Even more are home and friendship founded on a trust that outruns sight.

Where would we be if we first had to stop and prove? We should be like the distracted centipede of Carolyn Wells's lines who couldn't move because he could not prove which of his hundred legs should lead off.

> "The centipede was happy quite,
>   Until the frog for fun
> Said, 'Pray, which leg comes after which?'
> This wrought him up to such a pitch,
> He fell distracted in a ditch
>   Considering how to run."

Curiously, men who act constantly and everywhere else on faith raise this objection when they come to religion and belief in God. So Mr. John Dewey in his books, *The Quest for Certainty* and *A Common Faith,* insists that we ought to be religious without accepting any religion, that is, without having any belief in God, since we can never have proof and certainty here. But Mr. Dewey himself in the moral-social realm is definitely idealistic, that is, he believes in realities and values which he cannot see, in higher goods which men should set as the goal of life, in such social forces as truth and justice and good will to which we must appeal in the democratic method which he so ardently espouses, and in men themselves as rational and moral beings who will respond to such appeal. But if we have the right to believe on all other levels, why not on that of religion? The principle is clear: no life without trust and action. The higher you rise in the plane, the more inevitable is the necessity. Why, then, refuse this at the highest? The right to live is more than the right to exist; it is the right to live at the fullest and best, and religion alone can give that.

2. *Religious faith is neither illogical nor irrational; it is, in fact, faith in the rational in the highest sense of that term., The word "rational" has a double meaning. In understanding the reason, or explanation of any event, we first look backward; we try to find the antecedent cause, to account for it by something that went before. Thus we explain the automobile moving down the street by reference to gasoline, ignition, cylinders, transmission, and the rest. But we find a reason, or explanation, also by looking ahead. The car moves down the street because of the purpose of the driver. The car itself is explained by the fact that engineer and manufacturer had such an end in view. No world is truly rational in which what happens has not an orderly connection with what went before, with some "cause." But in its most important sense, the rational concerns ends and not just causes, what lies ahead and not merely what lies behind. No world is rational in which what happens is not in some real way

related to ends in view, to goods and goals which are to be realized. Scientific faith believes in the former kind of rationality. Religious and moral faith believes in the latter. If either were lacking, we should have an irrational world, chaotic and crazy.

3. Religious faith is not something apart from experience or devoid of knowledge any more than it is devoid of the rational. It springs from human experience on its higher levels. It is the confidence that this experience and its insights are as trustworthy as the information of our senses, while yielding us far more significant knowledge; and it is the determination to act upon this conviction.

4. Finally, it must be made plain that religious faith, like all other faith, requires criticism and scrutiny. Both religionists and critics are often wrong here. Faith does not mean wishful thinking. We have no right to say, "I need this kind of a God, therefore I will believe in such a God." Least of all does it mean the right to spin out our own theories. In religion, as in science, faith should be the response to an actual world. It is simply a response which trusts our insights and inner convictions as we experience this world. But, as in science so in religion, we must constantly apply certain tests and ask certain questions. (1) Will our religious convictions stand criticism? Have we drawn our conclusions rightly? (2) Do our religious convictions hang together among themselves? And do they fit in with the truths that we gain elsewhere? (3) Are they confirmed by further experience, as we put them to the test of life? That is, we must apply the three tests of rational criticism, coherence, and experi-

ment. Only, these must follow; the business of living cannot wait till all this is settled. Our real danger is not credulity but lack of courage. Religion needs reflection, but its great demand is high adventure.

QUESTIONS FOR DISCUSSION

What do we mean by "proof"? What different kinds of proof are there?

In the field of human experience and belief, what matters are subject to proof?

Set down any important matters where you believe and act but cannot offer strict proof. What right have you in these cases to proceed with belief and action?

List in order what you consider the best grounds for belief in God.

FOR FURTHER READING

In addition to the works cited with Chapters II and III, the following may be consulted:

W. A. Brown: *Pathways to Certainty*
G. A. Buttrick: *The Christian Fact and Modern Doubt*
Eleanor Rowland Wembridge: *The Right to Believe*
W. M. Horton: *Theism and the Modern Mood*
B. H. Streeter and others: *Reality; Adventure*
A. C. Knudson: *The Philosophy of Personalism*
D. C. Macintosh: *The Reasonableness of Christianity*
John Baillie: *The Interpretation of Religion*
Edwin Lewis: *God and Ourselves*
F. J. McConnell: *Christian Certainty*
H. P. Van Dusen: *The Plain Man Seeks for God*
John Dewey: *A Common Faith; The Quest for Certainty*

V

SCIENCE AND RELIGION

I. SCIENCE IN THE MODERN WORLD

OURS has been called an age of science, and the reasons are obvious, whether we regard the world of knowledge or that of everyday life.

1. Modern science has not only brought a marvelous advance in every field of knowledge; it has given us a new world. It has shown us a universe of unimaginable size, stars so distant that it takes millions of years for the light by which we see them to reach our earth, although light travels so fast that a ray would move around our earth seven times in one second. It has taken the earth from the central place that our fathers gave it and made it a tiny bit of matter circling around a particular sun. It reveals our sun as but one of thousands of millions in the particular system to which we belong, and then declares that there are many millions of such systems. It has stretched the bounds of time so that our earth, though a late arrival on the scene, is a possible two thousand million years old. It has studied atom and living cell and has shown us the world of the inconceivably small that surpasses, if possible, the wonders of the heavens above. It has banished forever the idea of dead, inert matter, and has given us a universe of throbbing energies. And this world of atom and chemical element, of living forms and starry systems has come to be by slow development through un-

numbered ages and is in constant process of change. The old picture of a completed world, finished at a stroke, fixed in its forms alike of matter and life, is gone forever.

2. Science stands for a way of study and an attitude of mind. To leave theories and prejudices to one side, to bring an open mind and ask only for the truth, to study concrete facts with endless patience, to try to find an order of behavior in the world (natural law) as indicated by these facts, to test these findings by experiment and more facts—this is the spirit and method of science. And in this teachableness of spirit, this openness of mind and supreme devotion to truth, there is something truly religious.

3. Modern science has had immense practical results. It is this that has most impressed the common man. For the man on the street science means the automobile, the radio, telephone, telegraph, airplane, invention and machinery, chemistry in industry, mass production, and all the conveniences and luxuries of our day. It is science that has transformed modern life. It represents the knowledge by which we control the forces of our world and make them serve us. Science means power.

II. THE SERVICE OF SCIENCE

No one can question the immense service which science has rendered man. It has destroyed superstitions by showing that ours is a world of order. It has banished ancient fears: think of the panic caused by the eclipse of the sun or the approach of a comet, of the dread invoked by illusions like ghosts and witchcraft with the cruelties which the latter called forth, of the pall of helpless fear that came with the medieval plagues. Think of the sufferings it has removed through advance in medicine, surgery, sanitation, hygiene, and a sane treatment of mental illness. Consider how its machines have lightened human drudgery and lifted age-old burdens from the backs of men.

And science serves religion. Its spirit has helped to remove dogmatism, the closed mind that was content with the past, the fear of truth. It has aided in correcting wrong opinions in religion. Faith sees the world of the unseen, believes that it is good and trusts it; that is, it believes in God. But faith is not necessarily right in the forms in which it is expressed. It may take those forms from the science of its day, and a later science may be needed to correct them. So religious men once believed that the earth was flat and the center of the universe, that the universe was made at one time and was only six thousand years old, and that the various forms of life were all separately created at the same time. Part of this was due to a mistaken conception about the nature of the Bible. The new science corrected the mistakes of the old science which religion had used, and historical criticism helped to correct the wrong idea of the Bible. Religion gives us faith in a living God at work in the world; science helps us to understand how God works. The truth that it makes known is the truth of God, and the laws that it discloses are the ways of God. It is this kinship that Alfred Noyes suggests in his *Watchers of the Skies:*

"What is all science, then,
But pure religion, seeking everywhere
The true commandments and through many forms
The eternal Power that binds all worlds in one?
It is man's age-long struggle to draw near
His Maker, learn his thoughts, discern his law."

We have been using the word "science" in its broader sense as meaning not merely natural science but all ordered knowledge. That includes history, psychology, sociology, economics. Religion is concerned with the whole man. The spiritual life is not a thing apart; it roots in our physical, mental, social, political, and economic life. Clearly, at all these points we must have help from science if life on earth is to be peaceful, wholesome, healthy, and complete. If there can be at one time five million youth in this country between fifteen and twenty-five who are neither at work nor in school, as was said to be the case in 1935, then clearly in such demoralizing conditions the religious welfare of these youth is involved as well as the economic. If there are more people in hospitals and institutions today because of mental disorders or difficulties than for all other reasons, then, though religion may have a large part to play here, it is highly probable that we need also a better knowledge of man's inner life and its ways. That is, religion needs economics and psychology. And it needs equally a better understanding of education and how to use it.

III. SCIENCE AND THE KNOWLEDGE OF GOD

Impressed by what science has done, many have hailed it as the one thing needed, as a very messiah, while others have declared that in the light of science religion is not only useless but impossible, since science gives the only true knowledge and science knows nothing of God. So we must inquire more closely what science is and does, and how religion and science are related.

When these claims are made for science, men usually have natural science in mind, the science which deals with the world of things. But to assume that this is the only world is to beg the question. There is a world of the spirit as well as a world of sense. Natural science includes only a part of our world. It purposely leaves to one side the world of person and spirit, of meanings and values. It does not ask whence our world came, nor what the true goods are for which men should live, nor the end for which this world exists. And more and more the great scientists see that science cannot even tell us what the real nature of the material world is, but can only describe how it appears to us and how it behaves.

But while natural science does not deal with this world of the spirit, it rests back upon it, it points to it, and leads us to its very door. It reveals a beauty that is everywhere in nature. It assumes that nature is something that can be understood by the mind and expressed in terms of thought; that is, that it has a quality of reason to it. It has made possible for us a larger and nobler vision of God. Too often the God of the older faith was one who stood outside his world, who created and controlled by some easy word of power which secured its ends at once and without cost. The world that science shows us today is one that has come to be through the patient, toilsome, painful struggle of the ages. If there be a Creator God, if all this is no mere blind process but a Purpose working to high ends, then we must envisage a God who is present in the world's life, who shares its labor and suffering.

We must note too that there are other ways of knowing than that of science. These ways are not so easy. I can weigh a man on the scales more easily than I can discern the spirit that is in him; I can measure a country's crops more readily than I can appraise its character. A seismograph may register the tremors of an earthquake more quickly than a man can apprehend the voice of the Eternal. But we *can* know the spiritual world, and there are other roads to knowledge than the use of test tubes and scales. Meditation, spiritual insight, faith, love, sympathy, moral obedience—these are some ways by which we may know the world of the spirit in man and God. There are doors to high reality, closed to our weighing and dissecting and testing, which open when we come with a humble and contrite and yet aspiring spirit. To say that there is nothing but the world of things is like declaring that there is no light when your eyes are closed.

IV. SCIENCE AND RELIGION IN THE LIFE OF MEN

Our principal problem, however, when we talk of religion and science is not that of knowledge but of life. We have seen how great service science has rendered to man, but the idea that science is to be the saviour of men and that nothing else is needed has been pretty well destroyed by the World War and the following years. Never had science put such tools into the hands of men. There were the new marvels of communication, the modern press, telephone, telegraph, and radio; the governments of earth used them to deceive their own and other peoples, to conceal truth, to spread lies, to create suspicion, prejudice, hatred, and fear, just as they are being busily used for this purpose all over the world today. Chemistry had made incredible advance; the nations drafted the scientists to create ever more destructive explosives, and deadly gases with which to wipe out not only armies but whole cities with their noncombatant population. Man's last conquest had been that of the air and this achievement has served, in connection with explosives and gases, to give the last and most terrible threat to human security.

But war is not the only scene that shows how science may destroy as well as serve, create problems as well as solve them. That is equally clear in industry. There we see science giving rise to invention, machinery, engineering, mass production, transportation, and enormously increased power. Yet the final result of all this in America, the wealthiest land on the globe, was fourteen million workers shut off from a chance to work, widespread poverty joining with idleness and the dole to work demoralization, while machines stopped and crops were reduced in the midst of masses that suffered for want of housing, clothes, and food.

This is not an indictment of science; it is only pointing out that science alone cannot be the saviour of man. It is man that has failed, not science. Science can create power; it cannot tell us whether to use our machines to till the soil and produce goods, or to employ them to blow up ten millions of our fellows in a World War. It can help us to create wealth; it cannot tell us how to distribute it justly according to the needs of men. It can show us how to rule nature; it cannot tell us how to rule ourselves or how to live together in good will and peace. Science is a tool; how it shall be used is another matter. In terms of goods and power, humanity has advanced in these last generations with enormous strides; in terms of faith and moral insight and character, it has only crept along. It is like one of those unfortunate beings who has the years and strength and passions of a man, with the intelligence and character of a child. The result can only be tragedy.

What, then, is needed? Of course there are the social sciences which deal distinctly with man's life within himself and in relation to his fellows. But even the use of these sciences demands the drive of a high faith and the motivation of a right spirit. We need religion. Men need to be remade in spirit. They need remotivation, something to take the place of the old selfishness and fear and lust and hate. They need to have made clear to them the meaning of life and the goals for which to live. And all this means that they must have a vision of God and be brought into fellowship with him. Knowledge alone will not do, nor power, nor new plans for economic change and international relations, nor piecemeal efforts at individual reform. Only a supreme faith, a supreme goal for life, and a new spirit within will suffice. And that is religion. It is the expression of that faith, it supplies that goal, and it is the great dynamic for transforming men.

QUESTIONS FOR DISCUSSION

What are the principal changes that natural science has made in our world picture?

How has science changed our social environment?

What are the greatest services that modern science has rendered? How far can we hold it responsible for such evils as modern war, unemployment, and the like?

How do science and religion supplement each other in the service of men?

What has religious thought to learn from the spirit and method of science?

How are scientific knowledge and religious faith related to each other?

FOR FURTHER READING

J. Y. Simpson: *A Spiritual Interpretation of Nature; Nature, Cosmic, Human, and Divine*

Julian Huxley, J. A. Thomson, and others: *Science and Religion*

E. H. Cotton, Editor: *Has Science Discovered God?*

J. A. Thomson: *An Introduction to Science*

A. S. Eddington: *Science and the Unseen World*

K. F. Mather: *Science in Search of God*

William Dampier: *A History of Science*

A. N. Whitehead: *Science and the Modern World; Religion in the Making*

James Jeans: *The Mysterious Universe*

H. Spencer Jones: *Worlds Without End*

Joseph Needham, Editor: *Science, Religion, and Reality,* a symposium.

Bernhard Bavink: *Science and God*

VI

HOW CAN I KNOW GOD?

I. What It Means to Know God

"To live is to know God," said Tolstoy. "And this is life eternal," we read in the fourth Gospel, "that they should know thee." In religion the phrase, "to know God," has a special and deeply significant meaning. It is more than believing in the existence of God. Men believe in the existence of God because others round about them do, or because they have been so taught as children, or because it seems reasonable to hold that there is some such power back of this world; but this does not mean knowing God. It means more than knowing about God. I may learn a vast deal about people on the other side of the globe, facts that I have gained from books or travelers; but I have never been there and I do not really know these people.

This distinction between knowing and knowing about we must grasp clearly if we are to realize what it means to know God. In languages such as the German, French, Latin, and Greek, there are different words to express these two kinds of knowledge, knowing about and knowing. So the Germans have *wissen* and *kennen,* the French *savoir* and *connâitre.* We may describe the difference as that between the knowledge of fact and the knowledge of acquaintance. The farmer may not know the facts of chemistry and yet he knows his fields, the feel of the earth

74

when he plows, the response when he plants this crop or the other, the look of the fields on a summer morning or under the winter snow. The carpenter does not know physics; he would open his eyes wide if told that this apparently solid and inert plank was composed of swiftly moving electric particles, as far separated from each other in proportion to size as the stars in the heavens. But he knows wood, even if he does not know these facts about it; he has the knowledge of acquaintance and can tell you how it feels under the plane, how it behaves when he saws and nails, or when he leaves it exposed to weather. This difference is most clear when it comes to our acquaintance with some person as contrasted with knowing endless facts about him.

But someone will say, Is it possible to know God? He is invisible; no man has ever seen him. He is infinite; how can the finite grasp him? The answer is: We can know things which we do not see or wholly comprehend by getting into working relations with them. So it is with God. Of course we are not left to mere guess or imagination; though we do not see and cannot grasp, the Infinite touches our life. The unseen world is not something uncertain or afar; it is here in the beauty that thrills us, in the solemn splendor of night that awes us, in the love that calls us out of selfishness, in the high ideals of justice that command us, in the Power on which we feel dependent, in the Help that answers when we trust, in the presence of Christ as we bow with a sense of sin and rise with the courage to believe in God's mercy. God comes to men at times even when they do not name his name.

II. The Ways of Knowing God

How, then, shall we know God? There is one word which for many gives the whole answer—"revelation." Finite man cannot know the Eternal, they say; only God himself can give such knowledge, and this revelation is in the Bible. The word "revelation" holds a truth that we must not simply admit but emphasize. If you believe in a living God, then it follows that such a God will reveal himself to men. Christianity believes in such a self-giving and self-revealing God. The knowledge of God does not rest simply upon human search and discovery; there is a double search, God for man and man for God. And even man's search is something that is inspired and guided by God. So there is no knowledge of God that is not revelation, that does not come from God and through God. But revelation must always enter through human experience, and it is this human side with which we are here concerned. What are those ways of human experience through which God is known?

1. We know God by the help of others. This is the way all knowledge begins; life is urgent, our knowledge is limited, therefore we constantly have to depend upon others. That is not merely true of childhood; throughout life, in matters of business, health, politics, morals, everywhere we seek wisdom from those who know where we are ignorant. There is special reason for this in religion. We are not deserting the way of experience; we are simply asserting that we should use all the experience that is available to us, that of others as well as our own.

The insight into the Unseen, the knowledge of how God works in our life and how we may relate ourselves to him, is not easily gained by one individual. We turn to the long experience of the race, and to those men whose persistent search, deep devotion, and special insight have led them further than others. Here is a heritage, tested by the ages, the most precious single treasure passed from one generation to another. Here are the prophets and seers and saints; here above all others is Jesus. The best of this has come down to us through the Bible, but we use other writings as well that give us contact with such souls. The Church, with its fellowship of faith and love, of teaching and worship, brings this to the individual and makes it vital and appealing.

Objection is often raised to this. Do we want lifeless tradition, a mere knowledge about God instead of knowing God? And have we any right to hand over this supreme concern to others, inertly accepting and blindly following their word? But that is not what is proposed. There is a wrong way of using tradition in religion as elsewhere. The ideals and insights that we get from others are not a substitute for our own knowledge of God; they are a stimulus, a help to individual experience and discovery. Who has not felt as he joined in a great hymn, or read a psalm, or a chapter from the Gospels, that God himself had spoken to him? We do not receive passively; rather, our minds are quickened, our hearts are stirred, our eyes are opened to the Eternal. And what we thus receive from others is not the end but simply the beginning. These words are an invitation and an impulse to action. They do not relieve us of the need of thought or effort or individual experience; they give us direction and start us on the way.

2. There is the way of spiritual awareness. With many people, perhaps in a measure with all at some time or other, there comes the immediate sense of something High and Holy, of an unseen Presence, a Power that is more than man. Some would deny this, but perhaps that is because they look for it in the wrong way. It does not necessarily mean some thrilling emotion. Nor is it something apart from all else, coming as a bolt out of the blue. We may call it by other names—beauty, sublimity, love, truth, justice. It is these and it is more. It is the sense of something that speaks through these, more than the finite, more than the changing; it is the Eternal in the midst of time, calling us to reverence, awe, and obedience. Here is perhaps the greatest value of prayer and worship. The sense of the Infinite is easily destroyed; the clamor of things about us shuts out the voice of God. Our eyes stop with the surface, the changing world of light and color and form, and fail to look beyond. The press of selfish and some-times sensual desire leaves little concern for the hunger of the spirit and that which can meet it. We need the quiet hour, that we may, in the parlance of the radio, cut out the static with which our day is filled and tune in on the Infinite that is always wait-ing to speak to us. Worship gives this quiet, quickens our sensibilities, and makes us aware of God.

3. There is the way of insight. It is one matter to see things, another to see into them. Here is where poets and philosophers, prophets and saints differ

from others. All men have sight, not all have insight.
Sight gives knowledge, insight gives understanding.
What is real and enduring, what is true and meaningful, does not lie on the surface. "I have walked
with people whose eyes are full of light," writes Helen
Keller, "but who see nothing in wood, sea, or sky,
nothing in city streets, nothing in books. Their souls
voyage through this enchanted world with a barren
stare." Helen Keller, without sight, has won insight.
Here is a true way of knowledge for man. It is not
imagination or invention; we must look at the real
world and not away from it. But we must look away
from the piecemeal and see things whole; we must
see things in their relations and in their meaning.
And when we look deeply enough, when at last we
see the meaning and the purpose of the whole, then
we see God.

4. We may know God by the way of action. There
is a penetrating word in John 7. 17: "If any man
willeth to do his will, he shall know of the teaching."
A great preacher put the same truth in the phrase,
"obedience the organ of spiritual knowledge." In
the broad sense it is true in every field: there is no
knowledge without action. The idea that we know
just with our minds is a curious mistake; the whole
man knows, and he knows with sense and intellect,
with heart and will. No one can really know who
remains simply an onlooker. Reflection and insight
and criticism are necessary—we must think; but
unless we enter into life, unless we give ourselves in
interest and action, we cannot know.

That is especially true so far as the whole world
of moral and spiritual reality is concerned. Men

have tried to settle these matters by speculation and debate, or by merely taking over the opinions of others. No man can ever know this world in such a manner. Unless you are willing to be a friend, with all the risk and cost which friendship involves, unless you are willing to give yourself, to trust another, to open your heart, to share your life, you cannot know what friendship means. You cannot know beauty by attending lectures on aesthetics or rushing through art galleries checking off in your guidebook the great paintings that you have "seen." You must give yourself in patience, waiting with open eye and discerning spirit, catching the beauty which the artist dreamed, or with hushed spirit rejoicing in the wonder of that silver line in western sky that marks the new moon.

It is quite plain how this applies to the knowledge of God—not to knowledge about God, but to knowing God. God is not an idea to be entertained, a theory of the universe to be proven, or a fact to be accepted like the statement that two plus two equals four; God is spirit, life, character. He is truth, purity, justice, love, righteousness, beauty, goodness; and "the character of God is known only as it is shared." The knowledge of God is morally conditioned. It makes a demand such as no other kind of knowledge makes. Let us see what it involves.

(1) Singleness of purpose and sincerity of spirit are the first requisites according to Jesus. This is the "higher righteousness" of which he speaks in the Sermon on the Mount. It is well, he says, to be honest, to keep from sexual immorality, to pray, to give to the poor; but more important is the basic attitude

of life that lies back of all this. And in two striking words Jesus shows how knowing God depends upon this underlying attitude or spirit of man. "Blessed are the pure in heart: for they shall see God." That is, there is no spiritual knowledge without spiritual kinship. An inner life that is impure is a bar to the knowledge of God; so are bitterness, anger, and ill will. The positive side is put in another and more striking figure. "The lamp of the body is the eye: if therefore thine eye be single, thy whole body shall be full of light. But if thine eye be evil, thy whole body shall be full of darkness." There is an eye of the soul, a window turned toward God and truth. If the soul has a supreme, a single desire, if man with all his heart wants what is right and true, then the light of God will come through. A pure and single devotion to what is highest is the first condition of knowing God, and not all clearness of mind can ever make up for its lack. For this inner eye may be evil. A man may have moral strabismus—he may be morally cross-eyed. But to look one way and walk the other, to want the good and yet hang on to the evil, to rationalize and sophisticate until we have made the good evil and the evil good, that is to destroy our one chance of light, to darken the window of the soul until "the light that is in thee is darkness."

(2) Moral obedience is the second way; the single purpose, the high aim, must issue in action. Moral obedience is man's Yes to the highest whenever and wherever it confronts him. Here is where the Hebrew prophets lifted religion once for all to a new level. Men had listened for the voice of God in

unusual occurrences in nature, or in dreams and
ecstatic experiences. The prophet heard it in the
summons to mercy and justice and truth: "Cease to
do evil; learn to do well; seek justice, relieve the
oppressed, judge the fatherless, plead for the widow."
Such obedience is not merely the act that follows
our knowledge of God and his will, it is the way to
such knowledge; and it is the way to knowledge
because it is the way of fellowship. "God is love,
and he that abideth in love abideth in God." Tolstoy
put it in a story, *Where Love Is, There God is Also*.
Lowell set it forth in his poem, "The Search." He
tells how he sought for Christ in fair nature, in the
places of wealth and power (since he was King), and
in temples of worship. Then Love came, he writes,
"and shared with me his crust," and so he follows
Love,

> "And in a hovel rude,
> With naught to fence the weather from his head,
> The King I sought for meekly stood:
> A naked, hungry child
> Clung round his gracious knee,
> And a poor hunted slave looked up and smiled
> To bless the smile that set him free;
> New miracles I saw his presence do—
> No more I knew the hovel bare and poor,
> The gathered chips into a woodpile grew,
> The broken morsel swelled to goodly store;
> I knelt and wept; my Christ no more I seek,
> His throne is with the outcast and the weak."

Conscience is not infallible, nor does moral obedience
insure correct ideas; but we cannot know the God of
love unless we live his life of love, or the God of
righteousness unless we seek justice in all our ways.

Here is a way that is open to every man. There

are many to whom mysticism does not appeal and who cannot accept the common Christian doctrines. To them comes the challenge of moral obedience: Face honestly your convictions as to what is just and good; be absolutely loyal in action to every ideal, to every least measure of faith that you hold; go just as far as you can. If you do that, you will know God, for this is his voice, here is his presence; and as you move on, the way will open before you. In the words of Novalis: "Moral action is that great and only experiment in which all the riddles of the most manifold appearances explain themselves."

III. THE CERTAINTY OF GOD

But is not this knowledge of God of an inferior kind as compared with the definiteness and certainty of science?

Let us note first that in the end we follow the same way of knowing in all the relations of life, whether we try to know God or nature or our fellow men. In every case we must obey a threefold rule. (1) Live, and see what life brings you. This is the empirical method. You cannot sit still and think and expect to know, nor yet simply accept what others say. Act, try, experiment, observe. (2) Reflect, interpret, try to understand what all this means. Use imagination and insight and reason. Our world is not a madhouse or a chaos; if so, life itself would be impossible. There is order here and meaning, and we must find them. So we have theories, hypotheses, beliefs. (3) Trust, and try all this out. Take your best insights and theories and put them to the test of practice. Science has no exclusive or superior way.

Of course the exact method will differ greatly according to the field in which we apply it, and so will the results. Each field of knowledge has its advantages and its limitations. When we deal with material things, we can measure and secure exactness; and the wonderful exactness of science has made possible the marvels of modern invention and machinery. Yet this advantage is paid for with a price; if you want such exactness, you are limited to what can be measured. I cannot measure the love of a friend, the beauty of a Rembrandt painting, or the goodness of God. Science today, grown modest with its advance, is quick to say that it claims no knowledge of what that final reality is which is within and beneath this visible world. When I come to beauty and truth, to friends and God, when I ask what is back of all and what it all means, then my scales and test tubes are useless. I have no exact formulae and tables to present. I must depend upon insight and faith; I must see what is unseen and value what cannot be weighed and measured. But I do see. I am still in the field of life; indeed, I am dealing with life where it is richest and most meaningful. Here I have found not merely facts but truth, the meaning of life and not its surface appearance, the enduring and not the passing.

And now we raise the final question: Is there certainty in this knowledge? Or must the life of faith be always haunted with doubt and God remain the great Perhaps? The answer to this is twofold.

1. Our certainty of God is moral certainty, the certainty of faith. I cannot see the unseen God or prove him with my logic; indeed, what kind of a God

would it be that I could see and prove? But the invisible is not the unreal. I know love and truth and righteousness; I cannot see or prove them, but they are as real as the visible world and more enduring. And to know them, to know their reality and authority, is to know God. I am certain of him, as I am of them, and I build my life upon this. Studdert-Kennedy speaks of faith as a great wager, but his words show that it is more:

> "I have looked into my mother's eyes
> And seen the light that never was on sea
> Or land, the light of love, pure love and true,
> And on that love I bet my life. . . .

> ". . . I bet my life on beauty, truth,
> And love! not abstract, but incarnate truth;
> Not beauty's passing shadow, but its self,
> Its very self made flesh, love realized.
> I bet my life on Christ, Christ crucified."

Here is certainty, the certainty that when we meet the highest and holiest, it is real, and more real than trees and rocks and hills and passing years.

2. Certainty comes out of life. In the end, nothing is certain except life; and life itself cannot be proven, it can only be lived. It is life that calls forth faith, life that brings us face to face with the unseen and works conviction within. It is as we act upon faith that faith makes possible the larger, richer life. And then it is this larger life that deepens and confirms our certainty. God too cannot be proven; he must be lived. And that is the final way to the certainty of God. All men are certain of the air, unseen though it is, because it is the very breath of their life. Many are sure of love and truth and justice because this

is their life in an even deeper sense. So others still are sure of God. He has spoken and they have answered. They have worshiped and the Presence was there. They have trusted and have not been put to shame. They have depended upon him and he has been their strength and peace. And day by day as their own life has grown richer and stronger, the light of this faith has given meaning to a world that without it would be an enigma.

Let us, however, remember two things. Such certainty does not mean omniscience or dogmatism; it is not assurance as to our ideas, it is certainty as to God. And such certainty is not lightly gained or kept; we gain it by surrender of life, we keep it only as we make life a great adventure and prove our faith day by day in new courage and devotion.

3. All this does not mean anti-intellectualism, the disparagement or doubt of human reason. Such certainty, on the contrary, rests upon the right to trust reason at its highest, not just when it analyzes, or when it asks how physical events are joined, but when it sees the world as a whole and the world at its highest, and finds in it order and meaning and ends which not only have their best explanation in God, but which demand faith in him. To deny this would be to deny reason at the highest. We say then with Walt Whitman in his "Song of the Universal":

"Give me, O God, to sing that thought,
　Give me, give him or her I love this quenchless faith
　In Thy ensemble, whatever else withheld withhold not
　　from us,
　Belief in plan of Thee enclosed in Time and Space,
　Health, peace, salvation universal.

"Is it a dream?
 Nay but the lack of it the dream,
 And failing it life's lore and wealth a dream,
 And all the world a dream."

QUESTIONS FOR DISCUSSION

What is meant in religion by knowing God?
In order of importance, what are the principal ways by which man can know God?
What ways have you individually found of greatest value?
What is the value of the way of tradition and authority? What are the dangers in their use? Consider the right and wrong ways of using them and compare their use in politics, economics, and ethics.
Consider what it costs to know God. How much do men want to know God?

FOR FURTHER READING

William Adams Brown: *Pathways to Certainty*
E. S. Brightman: *The Finding of God*
A. H. Gray: *Finding God*
Rufus M. Jones: *Pathways to the Reality of God*
D. C. Macintosh: *The Pilgrimage of Faith*
H. H. Farmer: *The Experience of God*
See also volumes by E. W. Lyman, Georgia Harkness, and others listed with Chapters II and IV.

VII

HOW SHALL WE THINK OF GOD?

MAN can put no greater question to himself than this. For this is not one question; rather, all the questions of life issue in this. What is real and enduring? What is the good that we should follow and the goal for which to strive? Has our world a meaning and our life a hope? Is there One back of the many, one Power that moves in all the myriad forces of our world? And is that Power Good? And does It know when we speak, and can we pray?

Along three main paths men have come to the idea of God: the sense of the Holy, the vision of the good, the discernment of order and end in the world. (1) The sense of the Holy we cannot explain, but all religions and all ages witness to man's awareness of something high and holy, a power on which he feels himself dependent, a sublimity and majesty that calls forth awe and reverence and fear. (2) The vision of the good opened man's eyes to a world that was invisible and yet real—the good and beautiful, the right and true—a world that stirred aspiration and commanded loyalty. (3) The visible world spoke likewise to his growing mind. At first he saw only the strange and awesome forces of land and sea and sky: the mighty tempest, the surging waves, the terrible thunderbolt, the majesty of lofty heavens, and, strangest of all, the mysterious power of life itself. But in the end he came to see that there was not only power in all this but order and unity and purpose; here was a universe, not a multiverse, a cosmos, not a chaos, a meaning and an end. And so there grew the vision of God, a being who was at once the ground of all nature as Creator and Ruler, the home of all truth and goodness, and the Holy One of majesty and wonder whom man could never fully know.

The Christian idea of God has its foundation in the Old Testament, its consummation in Jesus Christ. In the Old Testament the prophets give a vision whose loftiness and purity and insight we cannot appreciate till we compare it with what China, India, Egypt, and Greece had to offer. (1) There is one God, God of nature and of all nations. (2) He is the living God, not abstract idea, or impersonal force, or static order, but a purpose and power working out his ends in the world. (3) He is the good God, the God of righteousness and mercy. With an insight lacking to many even today, they found the clue to the character of God in the highest that man knew of what was just and kind and true. (4) He is the high God, the God of transcendent majesty and power, beyond all that human life can attain or human thought can grasp.

For the early Church all this had its consummation in two great convictions. (1) The character of God is seen in the spirit of Christ, the will of God in Christ's life and death. "God was in Christ." We see "the light of the knowledge of the glory of God in the face of Jesus Christ." (2) God gives men his Spirit. He is no mere distant God, touching earth but now and then. He dwells in men by his Spirit. But these two convictions form a unity: the belief in a Christlike God and in a Christ Spirit given to men.

How, then, shall we reach our own conception of God? The answer is fourfold: we will take the highest insights of the past, the convictions tested through years of experience, the supreme certainty of religion that goodness and power are one, the Christian certainty that the highest revelation of God is found in Jesus Christ. And four conclusions follow:

I. A PERSONAL GOD

God is a personal Spirit. The final reality in this world cannot be mere matter; science itself has repudiated that. It cannot be blind energy, for that could not bring forth order, beauty, and a life that rises to constantly higher levels until reason and love and righteousness appear. The stream cannot rise higher than its source. Matter cannot bring forth mind, though mind may find a place for matter. If reason and righteousness and beauty are foundational in this world of ours, then the ground of this universe must be a Person, for these belong to persons, not to things or blind forces.

There are those who think that in calling God a person we are dropping back to our childhood picture of a big Man-God in the sky, that we are making God in our own image, limiting him and dragging him down to our level. Let it be said at once: all our knowledge of God is partial and imperfect. We see in a glass darkly, and we have to speak of God in symbols taken from human experience. When we say King, Lord, Ruler, Creator, yes, and Father, we are using human analogies. But we do just the

same if we call him Process, or Order, or Principle,
or Cosmic Force. They are all taken from something that has come to us in our finite world. But
that does not imply that they are false. We can
know God because this world has come from God,
and we have come from God, and something of his
life is here through which we know him. We see in
a mirror, but the mirror does reflect.

What we need to do is to take the highest that
we know as a clue to the Most High. God may be
inconceivably more, but he is not less than this highest and best. Surely, he is conscious being rather
than unconscious process, reason rather than blind
impulse, moral being and not an amoral or immoral
force. So we do not limit God when we think of him
as personal. Rather, the limit is in us. We are not
so much persons as persons in the making, finite and
incomplete. Our wisdom is limited, his is complete.
We are bound to our little place; for him all space is
here and all time is as now. Our wills are faulty and
divided in aim; his will is single and sure. God is
not less than personal; he is personal life in its
fullness and perfection.

But while God is infinitely more than we, the fact
that he is Person and that he has made us persons is
of the deepest significance. It makes prayer possible,
for prayer is speaking to God as "Thou." It makes
worship possible, for you do not worship a process
or a principle or a blind force, but only that which
as personal and ethical can command reverence and
adoration and call forth aspiration. It makes fellowship possible, the fellowship of children with their
Father as Jesus taught it and lived it, not only in

communion of spirit, but in likeness of character and in common service of men.

II. A Good God

God is the supremely good. F. W. H. Myers was once asked: "Had you one question to put to the Sphinx, what would it be?" And the reply came: "Is the universe friendly to me?" If that question can be answered "Yes," then all other matters will take care of themselves. If we could but look up into the measureless heavens and forward into the uncertain future, and say in simple confidence, "Our Father"! If we could but sing with Whittier:

> "I know not what the future hath
>   Of marvel or surprise,
> Assured alone that life and death
>   His mercy underlies."

But that is the Christian assertion. Modern science has bid us understand the universe in terms of power. That power is the ceaseless energy that moves in atom and sidereal system, the order that holds the stars in their courses, the life that thrills in all living beings, the purpose that is working out in history— and that Power is Person, and that Person is good.

> "This world's no blot for us, nor blank:
>   It means intensely, and it means good."

It is important that we understand what we mean here by goodness. Various words have been used to indicate the character of God: righteousness, holiness, justice, wisdom, love. They all belong here, but the central idea is love, or good will. Back of God's creation and direction of his universe is this motive: he wills for his creatures what is good, and this good is his own life which he would share with all to the measure of their capacity. God is Creative Good Will. If we once understand this, we shall avoid two common extremes. There is the extreme of legalistic severity. God is conceived first of all as Ruler and Judge and law enforcer. He may be merciful, we are told, but he has to be just. Men are evil and deserve death, and God is under no obligation to save or help. If now he "elects" some to be saved, that is mercy; if he lets the rest go to hell, that is justice. But all this is to forget that good will is not something casual or optional with God; it is the very essence of his being. The highest obligation is there, not that of the creature's desert but that of God's own character.

More common is the other extreme, that of a weak and nonmoral or even immoral sentimentalism. The love of God is put down on the level of the softness and folly or even concealed selfishness which so often marks what is called love among men. But the goodness of God means creative good will, and each word in that phrase is significant. God wills what is good —not ease, not comfort, not just our pleasure, but the highest good of man, life at its fullest and best. And it is not simply the individual life that he wills: it is an order of life among men that shall be fair and just and merciful, it is a new humanity. And God works creatively. That may mean suffering for wrongdoing, it may mean toil and pain; but always its means a love that will not rest till it has brought forth truth, justice, purity, and mercy among men. And that can only come in a universe where moral order is as sure as is the order of physical nature without which we should have chaos.

Goodness like this, moral and creative, is more than a matter of the gifts of a divine Benefactor which we stretch out idle hands to receive. It is, rather, a life which enters, commanding and transforming, into our life. It means in particular these five great things: (1) a life revealed as our highest good and our true goal; (2) a judgment upon our imperfection and sin; (3) a demand reaching to our last deed and inmost thought, and commanding obedience; (4) a mercy that receives us into God's fellowship and brings a creative power into our life; (5) a confident assurance as we face the future that, despite every threat of change and evil, our life and those we love and all the high goods of humanity are secure.

The supreme expression of God's character is seen in the spirit of Christ. In Jesus Christ we have not simply man reaching up to God, but God come among men. Here is love that is infinitely patient, mercy that no indifference or selfishness or evil can turn aside, goodness which, just because it is love for men, flames as wrath at evil and is set with stern and inflexible enmity against that anger and hate and selfishness and oppression which curse and destroy. At the same time it reveals a God whose love enters our humanity, suffers in our pain, bears the burden which our evil has brought—a God who saves us by his presence.

III. THE GOD OF POWER

God is the God of Power. At no point is the popu-

lar idea about God more vague or crude than here.
Many have smiled over the naïve picture of God in
the play, *The Green Pastures*. There God is pictured
in a heavenly palace high above the earth. He can
wave his hand and create the earth and the living
creatures upon it; or, if he will, he can hurl a thunderbolt and destroy a race that has become too
wicked. And yet many people still think of God's
power much like this: he is an Oriental monarch,
with no law except that of his arbitrary will, and his
power is an external and irresistible force which
executes this will. They speak of omnipotence and
mean the power to do anything at all. They fail to
see that this is childish and irrational, as the small
boy's questions revealed who wanted to know whether
God could make a man fifty years old, or a stone
bigger than he could lift. Nor do they see that with
such an idea of God's power we cannot believe in
his goodness, for a God of irresistible power would
surely not be good if he left a world as full of evil
and unhappiness as is this.

We must first understand better what we mean by
power. There is no such thing as power in general,
no sheer power in and by itself. The power of any
being is its ability to act according to its nature,
whether it be an electric current, the wind and waves
of the sea, a growing plant, a laborer with his tools,
or a leader wielding the power that goes with clear
insight and high character.

So God acts according to the nature of his being
in its varied aspects, known to us but in part. We
see him as the sustaining energy and life through
which all that exists has its being, as the order which

makes this world a cosmos and gives to each particular being its own peculiar nature, and, finally, in his nature as moral-spiritual Being, as reason, wisdom, righteousness, and love. Some things are plain for Christian thought: all power is from God, all life depends on him, all that is good comes from him, and no force of evil can finally withstand him. But God himself is strictly limited, or conditioned, in what he does. (1) He is conditioned in power and action by that order or reason which is of his very nature, which is at the foundation of the universe, and without which this universe would not be possible. It is a part of this rational order that physical power cannot create the morally good. If God could make a man good by force, there would be no reason in the universe or in God. (2) God is conditioned by the ends that he sets: he must use physical forces for material ends, moral forces for spiritual ends. A kingdom of truth and righteousness cannot be established by physical force, and not even God could redeem humanity without the cross. (3) Finally, God is conditioned by his own character; his love and righteousness determine the way that he takes.

Our faith in the power of God is not belief in an irresistible force which God can wield like an army at the beck of an autocrat; it is the faith that spirit is more than matter and good is mightier than evil and that God himself is good. It is the faith that prays in confident hope and joy, "Thy kingdom come." Evil seems very powerful in the world today. It has wealth in its coffers, armies at its command, and no scruples to impede it. Its chief social forms are militarism, selfish nationalism, and exploiting greed. Justice is flouted, truth is buried beneath the lies of propaganda, and love seems helpless and hopeless. We read again Lowell's line, "Truth forever on the scaffold, wrong forever on the throne." But truth and justice and love are of God. They *are* God, God at work in the world. They are the final order of this universe, and he who goes against them, whether individual or nation, comes at last to destruction. Evil is self-defeating. A man with long years of criminal life behind him wrote his life story under the heading, *You Cannot Win*. The Caesars and Napoleons and Mussolinis defeat themselves. Love is mightier than selfishness, justice is stronger than oppression, truth must win out in the end against falsehood. It is in these that the power of God appears. Its symbol is not an army—that belonged to Rome; it is the cross, the cross which stands for self-giving love.

This does not mean a "finite" God as over against the infinite. It does not mean a God who is merely one among many forces striving for mastery. It does not mean a God who himself has "evolved," or who is just that "aspect" of the universe which furthers our life when we know how to adjust ourselves to it. All power is in God and of God, for all that is has come from him and has its being in him. He is the source of all being and the order in which all things act. But the power of God in our world is not that of irresistible force, but that of truth and love working in its own sure though slow way.

IV. The Farness and the Nearness of God

Theology and philosophy speak about the tran-

scendence and immanence of God. In simple terms
that means that God is more than the world and is in
his world. We may speak of this as the farness and
nearness of God, and in these two words almost all
that faith holds as to God can be included.

1. We believe in the transcendent God, the God
that is far; we pray, "Our Father who art in heaven."
We are using picture terms here to suggest spiritual
realities, but transcendence does not mean distance
in space. We simply express a conviction without
which there would be no religion. Religion arises
when man finds supreme power and holiness, before
which he bows in dependence and reverence and awe,
to which he looks in trust, and which he feels he must
obey. That is the God that is far, the being who is
more than the world of things and men which man
sees about him, yes, more than all the world of visible
things added together. We call this the holy, the
transcendent, or the supernatural. It is a God who
is more than a system of natural laws, who is more
than simply the energy that appears in floods and
storms and stars and growing life about us.

God is transcendent as power: the world has its
being in him, it depends upon him; he does not depend upon the world for his being. He transcends
it as purpose, directing its course. Through the
ages, from lower to higher, the world struggles on;
but there is a purpose that works in it and goes before it. He is transcendent goodness, rebuking, al-
luring, creating, calling us to worship and obedience.
Finally, because he is infinite and holy, God the
Eternal, he will always be other than man in his
nature and will transcend our human understanding.

2. We believe in the immanent God, the God that is near. Here too it is not something spatial that is meant. It does not mean merely that God is in his world, and it certainly does not mean that God is all things and that the sum of all things constitutes God. (1) The nearness of God means that God is not only other than his world, but is akin to his world, and especially to man. With all the imperfection in nature and all the sin in man, this world lives through the life that God has given it. "The meanest flower that blows" has something of his beauty and thought in it. Of man himself it is said that God made him in his image; and all God's dealings with man are on the plane of person speaking to person, of a relation with a being who can understand and obey and enter into fellowship with him. (2) God's nearness is that of his love and mercy. It is seen supremely in Jesus Christ, in whom God was present as truth and love and saving help. But it is set forth constantly in Old Testament as in New, especially in the thought of indwelling Spirit, the supreme expression of God's intimate presence as the very life of man. (3) Not merely in the world of man but in all nature there is, as Wordsworth's oft-quoted words suggest, this presence

> "Of something far more deeply interfused,
> Whose dwelling is the light of setting suns,
> And the round ocean, and the living air,
> And the blue sky, and in the mind of man;
> A motion and a spirit, that impels
> All thinking things, all objects of all thought,
> And rolls through all things."

Whether we think of nature or of man, we have no

right to think of this as a God-deserted world, or, however wonderful, as simply a world of things and men upon which a distant God, who once gave it being, looks down. Not for one moment could it exist without this Presence that moves in it and sustains it. And not merely sustains it—God is the creative power and the redeeming love that is always at work in his world.

In this paradox of the God who is far and yet near, the Infinite Spirit who is other and yet akin, who is revealed to us and yet beyond our comprehension, we find the spring and driving power of religion. Here is the tension that will not let man rest, that keeps his life from sinking either into complacent inertia or hopeless despair. There can be no religion except there be a God above us to call forth awe and reverence and obedience; but neither can there be religion unless there be a kinship which makes possible fellowship with him, unless he draws near with love to call forth trust, and with help to give us life. So in all high religion these two are inseparably joined. That appears in the sublime picture of God given in Isaiah 40. He is the God who laid the foundations of the earth, before whom the nations are as nothing, who created the stars of the heavens and calls them by name, through whose power not one of them is lacking. Yet it is this God who "will feed his flock like a shepherd," who "will gather his lambs in his arm, and carry them in his bosom"; who "giveth power to the faint, and to him that hath no might increaseth strength." And later we read of "the high and lofty One that inhabiteth eternity, whose name is Holy," who yet dwells "with him also that is of a contrite and humble spirit." And of the people it says, that "In all their affliction he was afflicted, and the angel of his presence saved them." (Isaiah 57. 15; 63. 9.) So, in Jesus' words, we pray "Our Father" to the God that is near, and find in him forgiveness and strength and daily bread; and in the same breath we say "who art in heaven; hallowed be thy name," and pray to this God that is far that his will may be done and that his may be the kingdom and the power and the glory. Here wonder and awe and submission, there confidence, joy, and peace, and both because we believe in the God that at once is far and near.

QUESTIONS FOR DISCUSSION

Of what value is a clear and intelligent conception of God? How far is such a conception possible? Do most church people have it? What stands in the way?

What grounds have we for thinking of God as personal? Of what value is such a conception? What objections are there?

What are some common mistakes in conceiving of the goodness of God? Of the power of God?

What does the idea of the power, or omnipotence, of God mean to you? What about the conception of a limited, or conditioned God?

In what sense shall we think of God as other than the world and as more than the world (transcendence)? What about the conception of God in the world (immanence)? How are we to conceive this relation? How are these two concepts of God related: the God who is other with the God who is like, the God who is more than the world with the God who is immanently and intimately present?

What are the values of these two conceptions for religion?

For Further Reading

H. F. Rall: *The Meaning of God*

R. L. Swain: *What and Where is God?*

J. Fort Newton, Editor: *My Idea of God.* (A collection of essays varying widely in viewpoint and value.)

F. J. McConnell: *The Christlike God; Is God Limited?; The Diviner Immanence*

E. S. Brightman: *The Problem of God; Is God a Person?*

W. R. Matthews: *Studies in Christian Philosophy; God in Christian Experience*

W. B. Selbie: *The Fatherhood of God*

H. Maldwyn Hughes: *The Christian Idea of God*

W. E. Hocking: *The Meaning of God in Human Experience*

Knudson, A. C.: *The Doctrine of God*

J. E. Boodin: *God*

A. S. Pringle-Pattison: *The Idea of God*

VIII

GOD AND THE WORLD

I. THE LIVING GOD

BELIEF in God of itself does not give religion; there must be also the conviction that this God is truly and actively related to man and his world. The thought is expressed vividly in the biblical phrase, "the living God." It means more than a God who exists; it is the God who moves in nature and history, who shapes and directs, the God who makes a difference. For many faith in God has faded out of life, not so much because of arguments against the being of God as because they do not find a place for God in the world. In the first place, they do not see any need for God: evolution tells how this world came to be, natural law accounts for all present happenings, psychology explains man's religious experiences as well as the origin of religion. In the second place, the actual world seems to them to rule out a good God. They point to the oppression of imperialisms and the rule of the sword, to the millions asking in vain for a job in a world where the capacity for producing wealth was never so great, and they say, as Israel's enemies said of old, "Where is your God?" It will not do to point to a God who in the distant past created the heavens and the earth, or who in some indefinite future shall come to destroy evil and establish the good, but who just now dwells in the far-off heavens. Nor is it enough to have a God

found only in the cloistered place of worship, or a
religion which is but the ivory tower of our hopes and
dreams. If we are not to merit the charge that our
religion is a mere "escape mechanism," we must show
men a living God here and now at work in his world.

II. NATURAL AND SUPERNATURAL

No little part of this difficulty has come from the
way in which men have conceived God's work in the
world. The battle has waged about the two words,
"natural" and "supernatural." Men pictured a two-
story world. Above was a supernatural world, the
place of spiritual power and perfection, the world of
God. Below was the world of nature and man, a
physical world under natural laws, a human world
under the forces of ignorance and darkness. True,
this world was not wholly independent of God; he
had created it, it still depended upon him; he might
reveal himself in Scripture, or answer a prayer, or
work a miracle, or live in the heart of a saint, or establish the Church with its sacraments as a supernatural institution. But even so, the supernatural
was a kind of intrusion from above, something thrust
into an alien sphere.

It is no wonder, then, that, against this piecemeal
supernaturalism, there appeared a revival of naturalism on the heels of modern science. For science could
do no less than seek to explain every occurrence in
this world as coming under some "natural law."
Supernaturalism looked for God only in the excep-
tional, in the gaps, and science kept closing up the
gaps with its explanations. So naturalism declared
that science was the only knowledge and nature the

only world. Both sides made the same mistake, assuming that where the supernatural was present, the natural was ruled out; that if you had a "natural" explanation, there could be nothing supernatural.

Let us now try to see where the real issue lies, looking with open minds at the facts. Ours is a world of things and of spirit. There was a time when men tried to reduce it to mere things, to matter and force, making all happenings a result of chance, seeing in all being, low and high, only chance collocations of atoms. But the very spirit of science itself, the open mind facing all facts, compelled men to recognize the presence of quality and not mere quantity, of values as well as things, of higher levels that were more than the lower—in a word, a world of spiritual as contrasted with merely material being. So the real question at issue appears: Shall we look for the explanation of our world in the material or the spiritual? Where is its real source and ground?

With the death of the old materialistic-mechanistic explanation of the world, there has come a "new naturalism." It accepts emergent evolution. It recognizes the reality of the spiritual; that is, of beauty and truth and goodness, of rational and moral life in man. But it still stands with the old naturalism "for the self-sufficiency and intelligibility of the world of space and time," to quote one recognized advocate, Professor R. W. Sellars, in his *Evolutionary Naturalism*. When the test comes, Doctor Sellars frankly declares that the world of things is the explanation of the world of spirit.

The other view is that of supernaturalism. Another word might be better since this is so commonly misunderstood, but the position is plain. The physical universe, with its order and beauty and its development from lower to higher, cannot explain itself nor the spiritual elements which have appeared in it. The ground and explanation must be found in a spiritual reality. The religious name for that reality is God. This spiritual (or supernatural) is not something in opposition to nature and outside of it. It is here in the world of nature. Turn anywhere and if you will but look deeply enough, you will find God. But the spirit that is in the world is more than the world. The "supernatural" is not a kind of spooky force working on the natural; the "spiritual" is not a kind of refined substance mixed in with the material. What we have is a Will, a Purpose, a Goodness, a personal God, not the sum of all things but their ground, their explanation, their end, himself always more than the world which has its being in him.

III. God in the World of Nature

God is in all his world, but men do not see God because their eyes are darkened and because they are looking for a miraculous force evident in some extraordinary event.

We see God as the creator of this universe. Of course, the carpenter idea of creation is gone. The Genesis stories are not a scientific account of when and how heaven and earth and life on earth came to be. They are the expression of a profound spiritual faith set forth in poetic form, the faith that back of this wonderful universe are the shaping purpose and order of God. We have nothing higher than that today, but we know better what the method of God has been. To call that method evolution is not to account for this universe but only to state the common theory that this world came to be by gradual and orderly change through long ages. Accept the scientific theory and the great questions still remain. Evolution could not take place except within a given order, or according to given "laws." Whence came this order? Whence came the energy that moves in this process? Why that urge that drives all things on? What is it that has worked so strangely to bring the higher out of the lower? Scholars speak today of "emergent evolution," or even "creative evolution"; through the ages there has been a strange tendency which one writer has called whole-making, another creative synthesis, another the principle of co-ordination. The lower comes together to form a whole, and the whole is more than the sum of its parts, is a higher level of being with new qualities and ways of behavior. So hydrogen and oxygen unite to form water, a compound wholly different from either, with strange and wonderful properties that make it a source of beauty and the indispensable servant of life. So the inorganic unites to form a living cell and the miracle of life occurs, life which in its qualities and possibilities and ways of behavior rises above all nonliving. What is this principle or process thus at work? Science does not try to answer; its task is simply to describe. But all this shows us God at work and how God works.

We may say, then, as we look at our world: God is the power that sustains all, in whom not only we, but everything, least and greatest, lives and moves and has its being; he is the order, sure and steadfast, which makes our world cosmos and not chaos; he is the creative Spirit, the life urge that impels onward, the principle of unity that is ever creating a new and higher order; and he is the redemptive Spirit, the great Self-Giver, pouring his life into the world.

In all this God does not work mechanically or compulsively. His way is the way of freedom. In Browning's fine phrase, God

". . . stands away
As it were a handbreadth off, to give
Room for the newly made to live."

He seems from the beginning to have dealt with his world as he now deals with man. He gives his creatures being and the urge to live, and sets them in an encompassing and sustaining order; but within that he leaves them to achieve. Creation means conflict, experiment, freedom, self-achievement. And for that reason it means trial and error, blind alleys like that along which the saurians moved who came to extinction because they were not fitted to survive. It means a price of toil and pain and loss, and long ages for the world's making. Yet this is God's way of working, and it looks more and more, when we come to deeper understanding, as though life could only be created by some such union of support and order and direction on God's side, of freedom and struggle on the side of the creature. Thus atoms and stars are included with living beings in one great process. Looking from above we call it creation; from below, achievement. Here is a sublime conception, far more consonant with the Christian idea of the God of self-giving life as revealed in Christ than the old carpenter idea. The Creator God is not force outside

the universe but Spirit dwelling in it, sustaining,
impelling, directing, but always as the order which
hinders evil and supports good, and as the self-giving
God of toil and love. Creation is thus one with
revelation and incarnation and redemption, all mani-
festing the God of whom Jesus said: "My Father
worketh until now and I work." And it is a continu-
ous work. Poets have pictured the glory of the morning when a new-created sun first rose in beauty o'er
the earth; but every sunrise is a new creation. As
Alfred Noyes has put it:

> "New every morning the creative Word
> Moves upon chaos. Yea, our God grows young.
> Here, now, the eternal miracle is renewed.
> Now, and forever, God makes heaven and earth."

IV. Concerning Providence and Miracles

1. The idea of providence is vital to religious faith.
To believe in a personal God who knows us and has a
purpose for each of us, to believe in a living God who
is carrying out his high ends in the world, this is to
believe in the providence of God. It is opposed to
the view of the universe as a vast impersonal order
to which man has to adjust himself as best he can.
It involves belief in a personal God, in the worth of
human personality, and in a personal relation between God and man; and these ideas are fundamental
to the teaching of Jesus.

Popular misconceptions as to providence have dis-
credited it. The belief has often been individualistic
and selfish. God has become a convenience for man's
benefit, and providence a perpetual interference for
individual advantage. But this is alike unchristian

and irrational. The Christian attitude is one of confidence in God's absolute goodness and devotion to his will. It brings all its concerns to God but it does not presume to decide what the good will of God is. It prays, "Thy will be done," and only after that goes on to say, "Give us this day." Its supreme concern is the purpose of God. In that spirit Jesus prayed, "If it be possible, let this cup pass away from me: nevertheless, not as I will, but as thou wilt." It does not presume to decide how God's good will is to be achieved, and its devotion to that will makes a merely individual interest impossible.

But even thus, guarding against abuse, can we still believe in a God whose love and thought and purpose reach to each human life? Is there a divinity that shapes our ends? Do all things work together for good to them that love God? Can we say "Our Father," or still repeat the twenty-third psalm and think of God as the Shepherd of our life? There is a line in Tennyson's "In Memoriam" that reflects man's haunting fear:

" 'The stars,' she whispered, 'blindly run.' "

Men are oppressed by the idea of an impersonal order that dominates all events, of an iron ring of law that binds God and man alike.

But this is simply the old issue over again: What is ultimate in the universe; things or spirit? If it be spirit, if it be a personal and good God, then the rest follows. To think of the "laws of nature" as an independent force constraining God's action is pure mythology. Science considers such laws as simply summary statements of the way in which things behave as science has observed them. Religion sees them as the order which reflects the immanent reason of God. Such an order is no more a barrier to God than to man. It is the friend of man making possible alike knowledge and effective action. It is the instrument of the living God as he works out his ends. God is not a prisoner in the world that he has made; he is the living, creative, sustaining Spirit, to which it responds. It is ours, however, in this faith not to decide just how God must work, but, as we trust him, so to leave all things to him,

> "Assured alone that life and death
> His mercy underlies."

2. As the idea of providence has suffered at the hands of popular religion, so that of miracle has suffered from the theologians. As generally conceived, a miracle is a break in the order of nature, an event pointing to God because "natural forces" cannot explain it; as such it becomes an evidence used to "prove" God or to authenticate a messenger or a message. But if this is what miracle means, then it ceases to be a religious matter and becomes an affair of the intellect, an argument used by a God who stands outside this world and has to depend on such external means to convince men. Today miracles of this kind have become a liability to religion, not an asset. The idea of external interference contradicts both our idea of God and our observation of nature and history. Everything hinges upon the explanation of just how this event occurred. But that is a philosophical or scientific affair, not religious.

We must begin, then, at another place. Men experience God in many ways, but there are events in which his presence and action seem to them especially and strikingly manifest. The terms used in the Bible for such events are "sign," "wonder," or "miracle." Religion as such does not concern itself with the question as to just how such events come to pass, but only with the conviction that God is working in them. One may think of an immanent God working through an order known to us or unknown; or one may take the old dualism and think of a God reaching in from without. That is a matter of theory, of philosophy. The crucial matter for religion is the conviction that the living God is here speaking to men.

The miracles recorded in the Bible must be studied as everything else in the Bible is studied. We do not accept a statement simply because it is here contained; each account must be studied for itself. Our first approach will be historical and critical. It will show that some of these accounts have better historical basis than others; that there is a tendency to turn spiritual events into physical happenings (note the way in which Luke "materializes" the descending Spirit in the account of Jesus' baptism, and the same tendency in his accounts of the appearances of the risen Christ); that in the main marvels multiply as the writer is removed in time from the event. On the other hand, it seems impossible to eliminate from the Gospels the story of Jesus' healings, or to account for the beginnings of the Church unless you concede the real appearance of the living Christ to the disciples. The second approach is religious and ethical. No accounts are worthy of consideration which deal with the trivial or with that which is on a lower moral level. Stories of floating ax heads, and of she bears which devour impertinent children at the demand of a peeved prophet, may be passed by.

The term "miracle" might well be dropped by us. The question has passed over into the larger matter, that of the belief in a living God, alike greater than his world and present in it, revealing himself to men and working out his ends. Not all is of equal import as evidence of his presence and power, but it is not the unusual and arresting which today has the most meaning for faith.

V. God in Human History

Does God work in history? That has been the problem of faith in all ages as it has looked at the suffering of the saints and the seeming triumph of evil. If we face realities, we must see that there are only two ways open for God's work in history. There is the way of direct action, the method of compulsion. Why does not God slay the sinners and put the saints on the throne? Or why does he not at least intervene in an exemplary destruction of some great offender? One can only say once more: that is a child's question, with a child's view of God as a big man standing above the universe, and of power as something external and absolute. Direct action can level forests or blast tunnels or drive slaves to build pyramids; it cannot bring forth truth or wisdom or justice. It cannot create men, not even a single flower. It cannot save the world. It is the same error that leads so many to imagine today that there is a short way out of our present distress by giving absolute power to "benevolent" autocrats. That is not the way of God. He does not save by "irresistible grace" (a contradiction in terms) or by force, which can only repress and destroy.

There is a certain analogy in God's work with what we know as the democratic way. One might better say that man is slowly learning the method of God. The old way was autocratic and militaristic. In part it rested on the idea that the common man had no real rights; that it was the divine right of the few to rule, the duty of the many to submit and serve without question or comprehension. In part, however, it was due to the idea that the masses were too ignorant to understand, too evil to choose, too weak to act. If we take democracy, not in the narrow political sense but in its broad meaning as a social faith, then it is opposed to this at every point. It believes in social justice and the rights of men as men, instead of in the privilege of the few, whether these few come to power by heredity, race, wealth, or ruthless seizure of rule. It believes in the might of spiritual forces, of truth, justice, and good will; and so it stands for education as against propaganda, for free speech and assemblage, and against the ways of force. It believes in men: not in their infallibility, not that the voice of the people is the voice of God, but that in the end, with education and full discussion, after trial and even mistakes and failures, the many can better be trusted in their intelligence and sense of justice than the few with all the dangers that come from vested privilege and unlimited power. But more than that: what the social order needs is truth and justice, and these not simply in laws but in the minds and hearts and will of the people. There is no social good, no social salvation, except as the people themselves are lifted to these levels. The process is slow and costly, but it is the only way.

This is God's way: truth making its gradual advance over ignorance and prejudice; love taking in community, nation, and other classes, races, and peoples in slowly widening circles; justice in law and industry as in individual relations; service as a motive above selfishness; and back of all and in all, a growing vision of God answered by man's faith and devotion.

God's work in the world is seen in his judgment upon evil and his support of the good. That is true though his thunderbolts do not strike down the enemies of men nor his intervention put saints on the throne. There is a basic order in this universe, beginning on the physical level, which works against isolation and separation and for unity and co-operation. It is the law of individual survival and of the emergence of higher levels in evolution. Unity and co-operation mean life, individualism and isolation bring death. Socially there must be mutual confidence, regard, and good will, bringing truth and justice. These laws of life are as sure as those by which the heavens stand, though their operation is seen only as we take the long look. Falsehood succeeds for a while—so did the propaganda used on all sides in the World War, just as it is used in Fascist states today, where truth is suppressed and whole peoples are supplied with ready-made beliefs. But falsehood in the end destroys confidence and so destroys itself. It is so with armed force—it never yet won a permanent victory. The opposites of truth and love and justice are error, selfishness, exploitation; they make for disintegration and self-destruction as surely as night follows day. The stars in their courses are fighting against Sisera, but he who builds on truth and love has on his side the eternal forces of this universe and its immutable laws. The universe has a moral character revealing the presence of God.

This principle is slowly becoming plain in the world of wealth and work. We all know there is something basically wrong in a land where nature offers plenty and yet millions are not merely wretchedly poor, but have not even a chance to work. Economists have been pointing out what has happened. The control of the sources of wealth is in the hands of a comparatively small group. Its plan has been, after allotting to labor and management the necessary minimum, to keep all the balance for itself. Had the profits been widely and justly distributed, the masses would have had increased power to buy. Instead, the profits were put back into more factories with which to produce more goods and make more profits. But the inexorable law of God works here also: selfishness means death. The failure to distribute decreased the power to buy, until at last storehouses were glutted, factories stood idle, and economic depression overwhelmed all alike. What is all this but the judgment of God seeking to show a better way to man. Sometimes this judgment comes in great crises; more often it works silently and slowly.

The power of God in his moral order works as truly to support the good as to hinder and destroy evil. As there is a self-disintegrating element in the very essence of evil, so moral goodness, because it is in harmony with a divine order, has strength that is more than of man. Of course that does not mean that the individual or nation will not suffer, but the movement of history is that way and the final issue is secure.

VI. God in the Life of the Individual

It is not so hard to think of God as the order of the universe or even as a general moral order; but there are many who cannot see how God can be concerned with the individual as such. That is especially true since science has revealed the size of this cosmos and the apparent utter insignificance of man. The individual man is but one out of a billion. The human race is but an arrival of yesterday. In his volume, *Worlds Without End,* the British astronomer royal, H. Spencer Jones, points out some interesting facts. If the story of the earth were written in a book with one page for five million years, out of the four or five hundred pages needed, there would be only eight lines for the time since man appeared, and only one letter for the whole Christian era. Our earth itself in turn is but an infinitesimal atom in the spaces of the universe. Were our earth at the center of the sun, the moon would be only half way to the surface. Yet if our sun were put at the center of Betelgeuse, which is the brightest star in the constellation of Orion, our earth would be only half way to the surface of that vast luminary. But in the galactic system, which includes our sun and Betelgeuse, there are some two hundred thousand such suns, and that system is only one of some seventy-five million universes within the range of our telescopes. How can the God of such a universe have any regard for this little creature man, and how can man ever presume so much upon his worth as to imagine that he has interest for such a God?

The answer to this is found at two points, the idea of God and the measure of greatness. (1) We need to have a larger conception of the goodness and greatness of God. The problem is not new. Long ago the psalmist asked: "When I consider the heavens, what is man that thou are mindful of him?" But his answer was not to assert the greatness of man but the goodness of God. At that goodness we can only wonder in grateful humility. And have we sensed the greatness of God? Are we not simply limiting God after our human measure when we think he cannot be present with his love wherever there is a single human soul? If God is present as energy in each atom, as beauty in the marvel of every single snowflake, as life in his myriad creatures, as sustaining order in this whole cosmos, why limit him and say he cannot be present as love where there are beings to love him in return? (2) We need a more rational measure for greatness, or value. We have confused size with value, bigness with greatness. Jesus held that a man's soul outweighed a whole world. His God cared more for a single little child than for all the bulk of Betelgeuse which is nothing but incandescent gas. Who is right? This whole objection is in part a lack of clear and courageous moral thinking, in part an effort to terrorize the imagination.

This does not mean that God is a doting grandfather, feeding lollipops to each hungry child, removing stones from its path, and incidentally preventing

it from growing into wisdom and strength and manhood. It does mean that we can say, "Our Father,"
and believe that God knows and cares. It does mean
that each human life has value in his eyes, and that
"every man's life is a plan of God." The order of the
universe and the vastness of the universe are not
here for their own sake; they are here to produce
something. And the highest in this universe, surely,
must be some creature who answers God's wisdom
with understanding, his purpose with co-operation,
his love with affection. And man can count not only
upon God's knowledge and love, and upon the fellowship of prayer, but upon help and strength for daily
life.

Questions for Discussion

The naturalistic theory of the universe and its inadequacy.
Where was the old supernaturalism at fault?
If we believe in a strict order of nature, where are we
to find the presence and activity of God in human
history?
How has the idea of evolution affected the Christian
idea of creation?
Where can we find the presence and activity of God in
human history?
In what sense may we call the method of God in history
a democratic method?
What can we believe as to the interest of God in the
individual, and his direction and help in connection
with the individual life?

For Further Reading

In addition to books listed under Chapters V and VII,
the following may be consulted:

H. H. Farmer: *World and God*
C. J. Wright: *Miracle in History and in Modern Thought*

W. Cosby Bell: *Sharing in Creation*
Rudolf Otto: *Naturalism and Religion*
R. B. Perry: *Present Philosophical Tendencies*, Part II
G. T. W. Patrick: *Introduction to Philosophy*, pp. 60-166
John W. Oman: *The Natural and the Supernatural*
J. A. Thomson: *Evolution*
Jan C. Smuts: *Holism and Evolution*

IX

GOD AND THE FACT OF EVIL

I. The Problem of Evil

"How can we believe in a good God in the face of the evil in the world? Are we not driven to assume either that he lacks power and cannot help, or that he is not good and does not care?" That is the hardest question that faith has to answer.

The picture that we face is dark enough. (1) There are the evils seen in nature: suffering, the pain that is a part of all life, the scourge of disease, and the tragedies of earthquake, flood, and fire, where blind and uncontrollable forces sweep men on to destruction. (2) There is the seeming indifference of nature. We read of the sun that rises on the evil and the good; but the obverse is also true, that storm and pestilence smite good and evil alike. (3) There is the world of moral evil, most terrible of all: man's folly, lust, cruelty, and greed, man's inhumanity to man. (4) There is the apparent injustice: the innocent suffering for the guilty, children for the sins of their parents, millions destroyed in war because of the wickedness and folly of a few. (5) And there is the weakness of the good, its slow progress, continually thwarted by the evil. Why is not God reaching down to smite the evil and set good men in places of power?

One fact bids us pause. The great spirits of the race, the men who have not just played with this problem in thought but have faced it in reality, who have fought the forces of evil with courage and followed the good with devotion, these men have believed in God and in the victory of the good, and have found for pain itself a noble place in life. To them we must turn for help. In the end we may find not only some ground for faith, but a faith that is richer and more significant because it has faced this question. In any case, face it we must. For the very heart of religion is here at stake, our faith that power and goodness are somehow one in this world, and that we can trust.

There are some answers to this problem that we must reject, three in particular that have often been urged. (1) "All evil, and death first of all, is punishment for sin," writes one. But pain and death were in the world long before man and his sin, and what kind of a good God would it be who could punish the innocent for the sins of others? (2) "All sorrow and suffering are sent for our good; their purpose is the training of man." But this does not touch moral evil; and suffering lasts on when no possible end can be served. (3) "Evil is unreal; there is only God and good." All three of these positions have some truth in them, even this last. God is the final power of this world; but, explain it as we may, evil is here. Even Christian Science, denying that evil is real, confesses its reality by the time and thought it expends in trying to meet and overcome it.

II. The Problem of the Good

The place where we must begin is not evil but the good. We take good as a matter of course, and wonder why there is evil. It should be the other way around. The good is the real problem for thought. What is the good? How can we account for all the good in the world? What kind of a world must we have for its making?

1. As to the first question, the good can be for us nothing less than life, life at its fullest and highest. The good cannot be anything outside of us, such as the things that we own. It cannot be anything negative, like the absence of toil and pain. The good means the good life: bodies healthy, strong, efficient; minds keen, informed, trained to think, rich in knowledge and wisdom; hearts broad in sympathy, endowed with patience, kindliness, and reverence for others; spirits with a vision of truth and beauty and God; wills that have learned self-mastery and can hold steadily to a high goal.

2. How can good like this be gotten? Plainly, it can never be a mere gift handed over from without, not even from God himself. Life is never something ready made; it can only be won through living. The wisest of parents, the best of teachers, can never deliver to a child wisdom or strength or peace; they can furnish sympathy, guidance, instruments for work, needed conditions, but the child in the end must work out its own salvation. When we stop to think, we all recognize this as reasonable; in any case we have to accept it as something basic to all life and being. As we have seen, it is God's way of creation: life through living, strength through struggle, knowledge by experiment, skill from practice, character through long choice of the good and living with it and being loyal to it.

3. So we face the crucial question: what kind of a world is needed as a place for man to achieve the good? Such a world will be a good world whatever toil and pain it may bring. And if it be not fitted for the making of men, then, though the skies be cloudless, though toil and pain and hunger be unknown, it will not be a good world. With many it seems to be quite taken for granted that they could easily design a better world. They are ready to say with Omar Kháyyám:

> "Ah Love! could you and I with Him conspire
> To grasp this sorry scheme of things entire,
>   Would we not shatter it to bits—and then
> Remold it nearer to the heart's desire?"

But what if the power were actually in our hands? What kind of a world would we frame if we wanted one fit for the achievement of life? Now, there are four points upon which the tragic evils of life seem to hinge. (1) Ours is a world of law, an impersonal, relentless order which treats good and bad alike, with no consideration for the weakness and ignorance of men. (2) In our world all are tied together, and therefore the innocent suffer for the deeds of the guilty. (3) This is a world of pain; suffering seems to be the one inescapable law of life. (4) Ours is a world of unceasing struggle and toil, where ignorance is always entailing mistakes and bringing tragedy. Why not then eliminate these in turn and make a happy world? The plain answer, if we will look closely, is just this: so far as we can see, no world would be fitted for the achieving of life that did not have these four aspects: order, solidarity, pain, struggle. Let us look at them in turn.

III. A World of Order

A good world, good for man, good for the achievement of life, must be a world of order. No other world
would be dependable, honest, or even intelligible. We
do not see that at first. The order of the world seems
hard and cold and unfeeling. Why does it not distinguish between the evil and the good? Why does
not this typhoid epidemic spare innocent children?
Why should not the cyclone turn aside when it comes
to the home of a saint? The ordered world which
science depicts seems so remote from the picture of
a Father God watching over his children of earth. So,
as William James once suggested, "there gradually
steals over us, instead of the old warm notion of a
man-loving Deity, that of an awful power that neither
loves nor hates, but rolls all things together meaningless to a common doom."

But what would we do at this point if we were
creating a world? Three choices would be open to
us: a world without any order, where anything could
happen at any time irrespective of what went before;
a world of piecemeal order, with some Power outside
constantly reaching in to interfere and make things
"right"; a world of universal and dependable order,
such as we have now. It is not hard to choose here.
The first would mean chaos, no possible world at all.
The second is almost as impossible to conceive. An
occasional interference would not do: for if God were
to intervene whenever there was suffering or wrong,
it would have to be every day in every place. God
would be a magnified nursemaid and, what is worse,
mankind would remain in perpetual infancy. When

once we face this seriously, the proposal becomes childish and impossible. If now we look at the third possibility, we shall find that that universal and inflexible order of nature that seems so harsh at times, is the first good gift of God, without which his other gifts would be impossible. Three points especially we can note where such a world of order is needed if human life is to rise above the brute level.

1. The order of the world is our first evidence that back of this universe there is a rational and dependable Being. Only in such a world could man ever reach the thought of a God who was both reason and righteousness, both mind and moral character.

2. Only in a world of universal order could moral character develop in man. The easy way for man is to be thoughtless, lazy, and selfish. We need not simply the high ideal to draw us, but the stern tuition of experience to drive us. If we will not learn otherwise, then the order of nature teaches us, "line upon line, precept upon precept." Under that necessity, lest we actually perish, we slowly learn industry, foresight, and self-mastery. That compulsion drives us to work with others, and so the whole life of fellowship opens to us. So the severity of God is kinder than the sentimentalism of men.

3. Only in a world of order could there develop reason in man, or would science be possible. No mind in man except as there is mind in nature to call it out! No science unless there be an absolutely dependable order! And without science, no invention, no machinery, no mastery of nature, no higher culture!

So the order of nature, that seems at first so hard and impersonal, becomes "the Godhead's most benignant grace." We see with joy that there is reason at the ground of things and something dependable in character. What seemed a barrier becomes an open door. It is an invitation to understand, an instrument for possession and rule placed in our hands, a way opened to higher life. Of this order of nature we may say in a measure what Wordsworth said in his "Ode to Duty" of the moral order:

"Thou dost preserve the stars from wrong;
  And the most ancient heavens, through thee, are fresh
  and strong."

IV. A WORLD OF FELLOWSHIP

A good world must be a world of fellowship, a world in which men are bound together in closest relations. We may call this the principle of solidarity, the idea of an organicistic, or corporate, as against an atomistic, or individualistic, world. We know how many and intimate the ties are that unite us: family, community, church, industry, education, recreation, friendship, and now more and more the wider world relations. It would be hard to estimate how much of the world's suffering comes in this way. Oppression and injustice, millions killed in war, children bearing the sins of their parents, parents suffering with and for their children, young and old, innocent and guilty united in a common lot of pain—all this is possible because humanity is organic.

But who would choose another kind of world? What would the human lot be if each walked his way, individual and alone? Again we deal with a law that roots deep in the very nature of things: solitariness is death, fellowship is the way of life. There is not one high gift of life that man can reach or hold in isolation. Love, friendship, honor, justice, truth, beauty, faith—all these come to us only in fellowship. True, there is a high life that each must live in himself and for himself and in personal fellowship with God: "the nurse of fullgrown souls is solitude." But we gain that life in fellowship with others, and we lose it if we do not from our solitude return again to this fellowship.

The answer, then, is not a world of pure individualism, if such a world were possible, and not a selfish life of calculated isolation. It is, rather, to open the door of life to love and faith and service like Him, "who for the joy that was set before him endured the cross." That is the meaning of the lines of the Irish poet, S. R. Lysaght:

"If love should count you worthy, and should deign
    One day to seek your door and be your guest,
    Pause! ere you draw your bolt and bid him rest,
If in your old content you would remain;
For not alone he enters; in his train
    Are angels of the mist, the lonely quest,
    Dreams of the unfulfilled, the unpossessed,
And sorrow, and Life's immemorial pain.
He wakes desires you never may forget,
    He shows you stars you never saw before,
    He makes you share with him forevermore
The burdens of the world's divine regret.
How wise you were to open not! and yet
    How poor if you should turn him from the door!"

V. A World of Pain

It seems most paradoxical of all to declare that a good world must be a world of pain, for pain seems the one pure and unnecessary evil. The least part is the physical suffering; the deeper anguish is that of the spirit, the pain and sorrow of the soul. Why not a world without pain?

Strictly speaking, the question here is not that of pain but of sensitivity. Pain is not a primary matter; we might call it incidental only. The basic matter is sensitivity, the capacity for feeling. Now, sensitivity is the necessary condition of all life. There can be no life, not even on the lowest level, without feeling and response. To live is to sense the world about us, to respond to it, and adjust ourselves to it successfully. Such sensitiveness increases in range and intensity as life rises in the level, and is highest in man. It includes mind and heart as well as body: there are worlds to which man responds that no lower animal can know. Of all creatures, his sensitive spirit alone is moved by the beauty of sunset and dawn, by the majesty of the stars, by the mysteries of death and life. He alone enters into the joys and sorrows of his fellows, and takes upon his soul their burdens. His capacity to suffer and his ability to rise belong together.

Pain, like pleasure, is never an independent affair; it is incidental to this sensitivity. That does not mean that it is unimportant. It may serve as warning, too sharp to be disregarded, and so save us from physical disaster; certainly, no physician would want to practice his art in a world where there was no pain to warn and guide. It may serve also in the world of the spirit. Helen Keller, who surely knew what pain and struggle meant, who fought her way out of the prison of utter silence and darkness in which her soul had lived since childhood, spoke out of her experience when she said: "The struggle which evil necessitates is one of the greatest blessings. It makes us strong, patient, helpful men and women. It lets us into the soul of things." Suffering "lets us into the soul of things," into the soul of God who suffers because he loves, into the souls of our fellow men. "Bereavement," writes Dean Inge, in a passage that grew out of his own sorrow, "is the deepest initiation into the mysteries of human life, an initiation more searching and profound than even happy love."

There will always remain a mystery to suffering, but one fact is clear: joy and pain are joined inextricably in life. The highest goods come by ways of sorrow and suffering, the greatest spirits have not won their insights along ways of ease, the great servants of men have known the cross.

"The cry of man's anguish went up unto God:
  'Lord, take away pain—
The shadow that darkens the world thou hast made,
  The close-coiling chain
That strangles the heart, the burden that weighs
  On the wings that would soar—
Lord, take away pain from the world thou hast made,
  That it love thee the more.'
Then answered the Lord to the cry of his world:
  'Shall I take away pain
And with it the power of the soul to endure,
  Made strong by the strain?
Shall I take away pity that knits heart to heart,
  And sacrifice high?
Will ye lose all your heroes that lift from the fire
  White brows to the sky?
Shall I take away love, that redeems with a price
  And smiles at its loss?
Can ye spare from your lives, that would climb unto mine,
  The Christ on his cross?'"

But there is another side to this picture. It is easy to overrate the amount of suffering in the world, particularly with lower animals. They have no memory of past pain, no imagination that sees it in the future. In their wild state disease is almost unknown, death is usually sudden and with little suffering, and there is little of that extreme sensitiveness that belongs to man. Further, sensitivity means capacity for pleasure as well as pain, for keen awareness of every kind of good and so for deep enjoyment. And even the simplest aspects of man's normal life, physical, mental, social, bring with them satisfaction and pleasure. Right living means joy in living because it means right adjustment within and without.

VI. A WORLD OF FREEDOM AND TOIL

No world is a good world which does not give man a chance to "work out his own salvation." It would seem so easy for a good God to provide a place where all our needs were promptly met and all our ways were plain. In an oft-quoted passage Thomas Henry Huxley declared: "If some great Power would agree to make me think always what is true and do what is right on condition of being turned into a sort of a clock, I should instantly close with the bargain. The only freedom I care about is the freedom to do right; the freedom to do wrong I am ready to part with." But Huxley's remark is strangely shallow for so keen a mind as his. We might sooner agree with Gilbert Chesterton's claim: "I demand the right to be damned." We must take our choice: which would we be, men or machines? Huxley wanted to think what was true and do what was right; but a clock cannot do either. If we want character (the "do right") and reason (the "think right"), they can only come in one way: we must have the chance to choose for ourselves, to learn, to struggle, to make mistakes, and then to press on again in endless effort. When Gilbert Chesterton declared, "I demand the right to be damned," he was asserting this principle that the right to be saved and the right to be damned go together. Name the high goods of life, for individual or nation—truth, freedom, strength of body and spirit, character; they can only be had by fighting for them. And each individual in turn, each generation, must win these anew; they can never be passed on to idle hands whether by man or God. There is no glorification of war here, or of a "rugged individualism" which means no more than selfish ambition and ruthless war taken over into industry; fight with others, not against them, and not with arms. So understood, however, Browning is right in his *Luria*:

> "Why, 'twas all fighting, all their nobler life!
> All work was fighting, every harm—defeat,
> And every joy obtained—a victory."

In his *Brave New World* Aldous Huxley has given us a brilliant, at times almost savage and indecent satire on that world of perfection envisaged by those to whom comfort is the great good and a machine made civilization the great goal. He voices his protest against this in the person of the "Savage," who had nourished his soul on a Bible and a Shakespeare that had escaped destruction by the new "civiliza tion." "I don't want comfort," the "Savage" declares. "I want God, I want poetry, I want real danger, I want freedom, I want goodness, I want sin." And to scornful protest he replies, "All right, then, I'm claiming the right to be unhappy." What is all this but to say, No world is good that does not give me a chance to be a man; and to be a man is more than to be a beast, no matter how warm and well fed, or to be an unthinking cog in a machine?

VII. Some Errors and Problems

Three mistakes are made again and again in relation to the problem of evil. (1) Men take the low view. It is not enough to ask: Is the world good? Good for what? It is not a good world for comfort, for ease, for freedom from risk and toil and pain. It is a good world for the growing of souls, for the making of men. (2) Men take the short view. They look at the moment instead of the end. But it is the end that decides, "the last of life, for which the first was made." We must "trust God, see all, nor be afraid." The world is in the making, the race is in the making, and so each individual life. And for the Christian faith the perspective includes the life beyond. With Browning's Grammarian, we

> "Leave now to dogs and apes!
> Man has Forever."

(3) The most common mistake is to take the part view, instead of seeing things whole. Men live on with little thought of their fellows, often with no concern for the larger world of humanity or the larger ends of God. And then when evil comes, they see

only their own loss. Over against these errors we can only say, If we are to have light on this dark question, we must look at the highest, look at the end, and see things whole.

Some specific problems will help illustrate this. Here are the great natural disasters which shock us again and again—storm and flood, earthquake and fire. How impersonal these forces are, how indifferent to distinctions of good and evil, how overwhelming to helpless man! But consider. (1) These forces are part of the order of nature without which this globe and life upon it would be impossible. The earthquake is part of that process of the cooling mass, the shrinking surface, the forming and breaking of strata, all connected with the preparation of a globe for life. Storm and flood all obey the common laws for wind and water and electricity, the working of forces in a system which makes the earth beautiful and furnishes air and water for life. (2) Every one of these forces represents an order which man can know and rule and use. They are our servants—wind and flame and water—if we will but patiently learn and faithfully use our knowledge. Often the evils are a judgment on our carelessness and selfishness and unwillingness to co-operate. The conflagration that made the San Francisco earthquake so terrible, the destruction of schoolhouses in the more recent Los Angeles quakes, both could have been avoided if men had built rightly. We know how floods and dust storms, drought and famine, are in large measure due to man. Selfishness, cupidity, failure to co-operate in social control—these have destroyed forests, turned into dusty plains lands that should have been left for grazing, failed to plant trees and control water supplies, and failed to distribute according to need—for this country has never seen a time when the harvests of the whole did not yield enough for all.

Or consider the matter of sickness and death. How tragic it ofttimes is! But here is no ground for charge against God. Sickness is not an accident and not a divine "visitation." What presumption to say that it "pleased Almighty God to take out of the world the soul of the departed"! Sin or ignorance may be back of this. Most sickness could be done away if science had the chance and society co-operated in using the knowledge gained. If you and I are not to blame in an individual case, it still remains: our life is possible only as part of a social whole and under a natural order. No man lives unto himself. We suffer together and we rise together. The piecemeal view can neither answer our questions nor show the way of deliverance. Out of this suffering, often of the innocent, there must come a sense of our social failure and sin, and a determination to work together for the overcoming of these ills.

Consider here all the suffering of body and spirit that comes from economic causes: unemployment, poverty, hunger, and that terrible feeling of insecurity that haunts so many men who cannot tell what to-morrow may bring to wife and children. Why should God let the honest and industrious and innocent thus suffer? Once more we must get away from the piece-meal view and see things whole. What God wants, what humanity needs, is a just social order. That cannot come by a divine autocrat setting right individual cases. It cannot come by outside compulsion at all. It must come from man, from a new conscience, and a common effort; and it can be made sure for individuals only as it is gained for the whole.

Upton Sinclair in his *What God Means to Me* tells of a man whose three children were killed in the collapse of a school building. Half crazed with grief, he would scream out his curses against God. But the schoolhouses were built according to plans which had no place in an earthquake area, faulty building materials were used, and back of both lay corrupt or inefficient government. This man of wealth, who had not concerned himself with this, or with the conditions of poverty and distress under which other men's children had to live, cried out because a divine power did not act as special guardian for his children. Paul de Kruif, whose earlier work portrayed glowingly what science had done for human welfare, writes with hot anger his book, *Why Keep Them Alive?* Science has opened the way to health and comfort and joy in life, he says. But vast numbers are shut out of all this. These gifts of science are for sale. The rich can buy them. Those with meager income, the unemployed with no income, must see their children do without them. Not in so many words and yet actually, by its neglect, society asks: "Why keep them alive?" The indictment stands against man, not God.

Back of all other questions, then, lies this question: If life at its best can only come with such cost, why should a good God bring forth living beings at all? The answer is: With all its pain and toil, life is good, and the God who is good wants his creatures to share it. So parents, thoughtful and loving, still bring children into the world. And men everywhere cling to life above all things; rarely, except when they have lost faith in God and hope for the future, do men leave life voluntarily.

VIII. Religion's Final Answer

It is a striking fact that outside the book of Job, the Bible offers no discussion of the problem of evil. It faces the facts fairly enough. The stark realities of evil, physical and moral, are nowhere set forth more frankly; the center of the New Testament, indeed, is the triumph of the forces of evil in the death of one that was wholly good. But Christianity is primarily not an explanation of evil but a way of overcoming it, not a philosophy but a way of salvation. We can only summarize this practical message here.

(1) No evil can ever separate us from the good. The highest good, and God himself, can never be lost to us if we will hold on in obedience and faith. (2) Evil is here to be overcome. There is nothing over which the spirit of man, by God's help, cannot rise triumphant. (3) Evil can be transmuted into good; we can be "more than conquerors." Insight, understanding of God and life, courage, patience, sympathy, heroism, all come out of such victorious contest. It is the Dante of exile that writes the Divine Comedy; it is the Isaiahs and Jeremiahs that, out of travail of soul, bring words of light and peace; the liberating words of a Paul or a John Bunyan come out of prison bondage; it is the Christ of the cross who says to men, "Be of good cheer; I have overcome the world." (4) Christianity points to the redemptive value of suffering. The cross is not a tragedy

but a triumph, not a defeat but a step forward in human redemption. The way of life on this globe from beginning to end is one of vicarious suffering: the family, friendship, the State, the Church, every human good is built upon it. Suffering is a challenge to serve; borne unselfishly, heroically, in faith, it becomes part of humanity's way to life. (5) Christianity points to a God who himself toils and suffers, who in all our affliction is afflicted and by the "angel of his presence" saves us.

Here, then, is a word for us to speak when other words fail. When a man is in the midst of the first great grief that seems to sweep away all his faith, at a time when reasoned argument has little chance, we can bring this Christian challenge: If I cannot explain this tragedy, I can show you a way out. All that is good in your life has come from God. When you have obeyed him implicitly and trusted him absolutely, you have never been put to shame. Do that now. You will find strength for each step and a light that will grow as you move on. Above all, you will be more and more sure of God, more and more certain that, though evil is here, God is here also, and God is greater than evil. So it shall be as with Tennyson's friend, who

> "came at length;
> To find a stronger faith his own;
> And Power was with him in the night,
> Which makes the darkness and the light,
> And dwells not in the light alone."

Questions for Discussion

Make a list of the kinds of evil which, to your mind, make it hard to believe in a good God.

Taking these evils one at a time, consider them in connection with the principles discussed in this chapter (a universal order, fellowship or social solidarity, sensitivity or pain, freedom and toil). Which of these principles, or aspects of world life are involved in each of these kinds of evil?

What is for you the most difficult point in the problem of evil? What consideration (or considerations) have given you the most help in this problem?

At what points would you change the basic order of the world in view of the evils you have indicated? (It is assumed here that we cannot have recourse to a piecemeal supernaturalism, with a God interfering here and there to make special adjustments; also that we must "see things whole" and consider what would be involved in such changes and what consequences would follow from them.)

FOR FURTHER READING

Leslie D. Weatherhead: *Why Do Men Suffer?*
E. R. E.; Articles on "Good and Evil," "Theodicy," "Suffering"
R. A. Tsanoff: *The Nature of Evil*
W. K. Wright: *A Student's Philosophy of Religion*
Consult also works cited with Chapters I, II, and IV

X

WHAT IS MAN?

IDEAS differ as much about man as they do about God. Where did man come from? What is he? What kind of stuff is he made of?

I. THE ORIGIN OF MAN

The Christian answer has always been very simple: God created man. Can we hold that in the face of modern science? Traditional theology built up its picture on the basis of the Genesis story: man was created perfect and complete, fully endowed in mind and spirit, some six thousand years ago. Modern science, on the contrary, thinks of the human race as having come by a slow process of development from lower forms of life, and as having existed anywhere from three hundred thousand to a million years.

When Darwinism first came, men feared that it would do away entirely with the Christian belief as to man. Three objections were raised: it destroyed the authority of the Bible; it denied God as Creator and made man a product of "Nature"; it degraded man to the beasts. The fears have proven false. The discussion has helped to a better understanding alike of what science can do and of what faith involves. (1) The Bible is not revealed science and history. Its authority is in the field of the ethical and spiritual; it shows us what God is and what man should be.

(2) To speak of nature does not rule out God; to hold to evolution does not eliminate creation. (3) A faith for today must hold to a God who is in all the life and process of nature as its order, its directing purpose, its sustaining energy, and not merely in some "gap" or special event here or there. What we have is a new picture of how God creates. (4) What man is is decided not by what he came from but by what he has attained. Every single human being was once nothing more than a microscopic germ in the womb. What difference does it make if the race in like fashion came by growth from some such primordial germ?

Just how God worked creatively in making man we cannot tell. The modern conception of emergent evolution, called by some creative evolution, recognizes that in the long process that prepared for man there was a succession of emerging levels, one rising above the other, but each resting upon what went before. The appearance of man was the great event in this long story. "The breach between ethical man and prehuman nature," writes Sir J. Arthur Thomson, the distinguished scientist, "constitutes, without exception, the most important fact which the universe has to show." He thinks that man "probably arose by a mutation; that is to say, by a discontinuous variation of a considerable magnitude." When the conditions were present, something new and higher appeared; that is creativity. Science cannot explain it and does not seek to, for its task is simply to describe the process. Religion sees as the only adequate ground a living, purposeful, creative God. This creative work of God is still going on, not only in the heavens above, where astronomy tells us of the birth and death of stars, but here on earth and with man. According to H. F. Osborn, distinguished anthropologist, the high point of man's "natural" development was perhaps reached thirty or forty thousand years ago in western Europe with the Cro-Magnon race which was the equal in psychophysical endowment of the highest races today. But human evolution has not ceased; it is simply going forward on other levels—social, cultural, spiritual.

II. WHAT IS MAN?

No one word can answer the question, What is man? Man is many things. He classifies biologically as a primate, closely related to the anthropoid apes. Bone for bone, muscle for muscle, organ for organ, you can compare him with the ape, or, indeed, with an animal like the horse. He shares with his brother animals many basic impulses and passions. Analyzed chemically, the average adult is composed of ten gallons of water, twenty-four pounds of carbon (coal, if you will), seven pounds of lime, one and four fifths of phosphorus, a half teaspoonful of sugar, with nine times as much salt, some oxygen, hydrogen, and nitrogen, iron enough for one large nail, and a few other chemicals. These are all facts beyond dispute, but the crucial question remains: Is this all there is to man? Is he a chemical compound or a rational spirit? Is he a sum of electrical energies, a particularly complex pattern of protons and electrons, or is he a self, a soul? Is he a mere resultant of mechanical forces, or is he a free agent who can follow high ideals? Is he a "high-grade simian, or a son of God"?

On the one side we have the naturalistic answers. They vary, but all agree that man can be explained in terms of the physical. Man is a mere sum of habits resulting from mechanical response to physical stimuli, says J. B. Watson, the behaviorist. Man's personality is the product of the endocrine glands, others say, moved by the discovery of the profound influences of the ductless glands alike upon man's physical and psychical being. Others apply the physical yardstick, like Harlow Shapley, the astronomer, who points out the enormous expanse of the universe and so finds man "in all ways small—inconsequential in every respect except, perhaps, in the chemical complexities of our mental relations." (Even a great astronomer can be naïve outside of his own field, as in this bland assumption that thought is a chemical process.) Harry Elmer Barnes, sociologist, finds in human history "nothing but the record of the responses of a bio-chemical entity to terrestrial stimulation." Popularly this is often just the revival of a crude materialism, which becomes a convenient way of getting rid of moral ideals at the same time. That can be illustrated by a passage from a best-seller of a few years since, *Twenty-Four Hours,* by Louis Bromfield. If we deal "with hard realities instead of the unwholesome putrescences of dead moralities," he writes, then we see man as "a piece of machinery, a bundle of glands and nerves and organs." If you fell in love with a lovely woman like Nancy, "there couldn't be any sentiment or romance because you would know exactly what was the matter with you. You would know that it was merely chemical. Men were simply insects of the most insignificant sort being driven by a tyrannical power along paths that had nothing to do with their own wills."

On the other side stand those who believe that man belongs to two worlds, the physical and the spiritual, the seen and the unseen. That does not mean dualism. It does not mean that the physical is evil. Physical and spiritual are both needed. In creative evolution, each stage, rising out of what went before, does not cast off the lower stage, but masters and uses it, taking it up into something higher. Life uses matter, mind uses matter and life, and spirit uses all three. So man is this strange mixture of body and spirit, of earth and heaven. So Fannie Stearns Davis writes of the child as

> "Made like a star to shine,
> Made like a bird to fly,
> Out of a drop of our blood,
> And earth, and fire, and God."

But it is this world of the spirit that gives man his distinctive character. From this world we have come, "from God, who is our home"; and this higher world represents our real life, our true goal.

Here, then, is a double peculiarity of man. (1) He is a creature of vision. That does not mean a visionary creature, for what he sees is real and enduring. The animal knows cold and heat, tempest and calm; man discerns the hidden order and reason that is in it all—and that we call science. Lesser creatures are all determined by instinct and impulse reacting to things about them; man sees goods that are unseen, ideals waiting to be realized, standards to rule his action—and that we call ethics. Man sees God—

and that we call religion. (2) But man not merely sees the unseen, he makes it his goal. He is a creature of infinite longing and divine discontent. Other creatures live only in the world of "is," man in the world of "ought." With man evolution comes to a new stage. There is now more than a blind urge, or an unconscious process. Creation comes to consciousness; the creature sees what it means and enters into the task. Reason is here, and God says, "Son of man, stand upon thy feet. Come now and let us reason together." Here is a will that can choose, and men become co-creators, "workers together with God." So begins man's endless search for a city, unseen and yet with sure foundations, whose builder and maker is God. Man lives in a world that is and in one that is to be. "I tell you," writes Shaw in his *Man and Superman,* "that as long as I can conceive something better than myself, I cannot be easy unless I am striving to bring it into existence or clearing the way for it. That is the law of my life." In Augustine's great word: "Thou has made us unto thyself, and our souls are restless till they rest in thee."

There are other things that mark man off. (1) He walks erect, with eyes that look up and out, and hands set free to shape instruments and use them. He is the tool-using animal. (2) He has reason, can form general ideas, can interpret what his senses bring, and so enlarge his knowledge as well as rule his world. (3) He has speech, not merely signs and sounds for particular things. Speech led to writing and so made possible a growing culture, a social heritage without which each generation would have to begin at scratch back in barbarism. (4) He is morally free. No argument of the schools has ever shaken that conviction in man. We not only choose but we know we might have chosen otherwise, and so we feel responsible and hold others responsible in law and in common life. We can halt action, reflect, weigh reasons, and decide. (5) Man is the most plastic of all beings. Of all creatures he is most helpless at birth, least formed, and with the longest infancy. But this helpless infant is a bundle of unmeasured possibilities. The chick can peck at its food and run about the day it steps out of its shell, but the chick can never be aught but a chicken. "You cannot change human nature," men say. On the contrary, says John Dewey, man is the most plastic of all beings. So progress, as Browning says, is

"Man's distinctive mark alone,
Not God's, and not the beasts: God is, they are,
Man partly is and wholly hopes to be."

"It is the nature of human nature to change itself," says Professor Hocking.

We might sum up by saying: Man is a son of God in the making, whose real nature is to be found, not in what he is, but in what he is to be.

And so we can understand the Christian idea of the sacredness of human personality. It is not a matter of how wise and strong and unselfish a given man may be. All humanity is sacred because man is a person and not a thing, because "person" means possibility and destiny. So man must always be treated as an end, never as a means, a truth that the prophets and Jesus asserted long before Kant announced it to the philosophers. Man belongs to God; he is to know him, is to become like him, to enter into fellowship with him and say, "Our Father." One human life outweighs the world in value. He that makes even the least child to "stumble" might better, after the manner of summary criminal execution in that day, have a stone tied to his neck and be drowned in the sea. Humanity is the end, all else is means; all else is here to serve: State and Church, the power of the mighty, the wisdom of the learned, the skill of the trained, the possessions of the rich.

The revolutionary meaning of such ideas appears when we challenge the society of our day in their name. One after another our institutions deny the Christian conception of man. That is true of Fascism, indeed, of all autocracies and militarisms. For them man is the property and tool of State or nation. The women are to breed children for its armies; the men are to create wealth and fight battles to enhance its glory, or to keep its rulers in power. And instead of men being free to think and choose and rule, they are to think according to a State-controlled press and obey without question or reflection. Our industry falls under like condemnation. The concern of God is not with the few, the clever, the mighty, the privileged, but with men as men. Are his eyes shut to the fact that in a land of possible plenty millions are shut off from land and tools and mine, from a chance to earn their bread? And is the Church free from blame? Are there not leaders who are more concerned about maintaining the institution than about serving men, and teachers who are more anxious about dotting "i's" and crossing "t's," according to theological tradition, than about dealing justly and loving kindness and walking humbly with God?

III. HUMAN NATURE: GOOD OR BAD?

What kind of stuff is man made of? Is human nature good or evil? What are its possibilities? The question is no idle one. It not only concerns religion, but all our social hopes and plans depend upon it. The answer will determine what we can plan in education and government and industry, as well as the possibilities of individual life. Democracy, for example, means faith in man, not the idea that the voice of the people is the voice of God, but that despite all weakness and failure, in the end, with education and free discussion, we can trust the intelligence and good faith of the rank and file. Autocracy, where it is not pure selfishness, involves a mean estimate of the common man. So in industry, if man is a purely selfish and materialistic being, then we may claim that a co-operative commonwealth is impossible and we must have a system of competition appealing to self-interest.

The estimate of human nature has been marked by two extremes, which we may call romanticism and pessimism. The first is the idealization of human nature associated with Rousseau and the romanticism of the eighteenth century. Human nature is good when unspoiled by artificial civilization. The simple savage becomes the ideal. To this idea of natural goodness was added that of the "law of progress," which was supposed to follow from the theory of evolution. The popular conception is well expressed by a passage in Andrew Carnegie's *Autobiography*, where he tells of his first acquaintance with Darwin and Spencer: "I had found the truth of evolution. 'All is well since all grows better,' became my motto, my true source of comfort. Man was not created with an instinct for his own degradation." Instead "man absorbed such mental foods as were favorable to him, retaining what was salutary, rejecting what was deleterious." The World War was the tragic answer to this philosophy of optimism, and because of it Mr. Carnegie's *Autobiography* was never completed. There followed the even more tragic peace of Versailles and the destructive postwar years. Before us stood the darker side of human nature, the forces of evil with which we had to deal in fighting for justice and peace: ignorance, stupidity, inertia, fear, credulity, prejudice, narrowness, selfishness, lust, cruelty, hate.

As a result we have a strong swing today to the other extreme, that of pessimism. We are asked to be realistic; what is meant is cynicism, pessimism, and despair. Man is stupid and incompetent, a creature of impulse and passion, not of reason and insight, and incurably selfish with no motive but his own interest. Such a theory has profound social, as well as religious, consequences. Holding this position, Fascism decides that democracy is impossible, political freedom a delusion, and dictatorship a necessity. Upon this belief militarism rests, for if reason and conscience are not available, the only recourse is war. And if man be essentially egoistic, then the dominant motive in industry must be individual advantage; hence an economic order based on co-operation and rational planning is out of question, and a competitive capitalism remains the last word, with the possible exception of a communism introduced by violence, maintained by force, and divorced from democracy.

But is not this conception of human nature the orthodox Christian view? To answer this we must consider the traditional idea of the fall and total depravity. The Genesis story of the temptation and fall, like that of the creation, is of profound and lasting significance. It was one of the early attempts to face the fact of evil and reconcile it with the goodness of God. Evil is here, says the writer, but it is man's choosing, not God's making. Into this story, which receives but one other mention in the Bible, later theology read its own ideas. The extreme position is that of Augustine and Calvin. Human nature before the fall, they held, was holy and faultless. Adam's one choice at once transformed him and the whole race, which was "in Adam," so that human nature became utterly evil and corrupt. In Calvin's words: "The whole man, from the crown of the head to the sole of the foot, is so deluged, as it were, that no part remains exempt from sin." Even of newborn infants he says: "Their whole nature is a seed-bed of sin, and therefore cannot but be odious and abominable to God." So these infants, even before they can know or choose, suffer "for their own defects, bringing their condemnation from their mother's womb," which means that newborn infants, dying, might as sinners be justly sent to hell.

We can appreciate the underlying motives of Augustine and Calvin. They wanted men to see the blackness of sin against the holiness of God, and to realize its terrible results. They wished to emphasize the grace of God and man's utter dependence. But Calvin's actual doctrine was a caricature of reality and a departure from the Christian idea. It pictures man as he might be in a world of sin wholly separated from God and good. But humanity is not thus deserted by God, and there is no human nature like this outside the theologian's closet. What this idea of man leads to is seen when we come to Calvin's doctrine of salvation. If man is this utterly evil thing, lacking all vision of God, all desire for good, all capacity to respond, then he is no longer a moral person, but a mere thing, inert and impotent. Then salvation will have to be a one-way affair, every step of which is determined by God and God alone. Hence, necessarily, it is God and God alone that decides who is to be saved and who is to be damned; and those who are chosen are saved by a power which they can neither resist nor escape ("irresistible grace" and "the perseverance of the saints"). Salvation, in effect, becomes a mechanical rather than a moral process. And when we consider what Calvin himself calls "the horrible decree," by which God determines in advance who shall be saved and who damned, we see how sovereign power is exalted above character in God, and how his justice and mercy are impugned.

If, now, we turn to the Bible, especially the New Testament, we are struck with the extraordinary way in which it unites severity and hopefulness, realism and idealism. Nowhere do you find so severe a judgment on man, such insight into the depths of human evil, such uncompromising judgment. There is certainly no superficial romanticism here, no happy optimism about a human nature that is essentially good and always growing better. Jesus "knew what was in man," and in his life and death he learned what fickleness, indifference, hatred, fear, and selfish cruelty could do. In his work Paul dealt with the dregs of the Roman world. He knew at first hand the big cities like Corinth and Rome—the Rome that was called "the big sewer," into which all the filth of the empire flowed, the Corinth which supplied the word "corinthianize" as a symbol of profligacy. No Roman satirist ever painted a blacker picture than Paul gives in those first chapters of his letter to the Romans. Writing to the Corinthian church he gives a list of reprobates—thieves, drunkards, extortioners, fornicators, and then adds: "And such were some of you."

But even more extraordinary is the other side, the faith and high expectation which the New Testament shows in relation to man. That does not, of course, appear in abstract statement or theory—the New Testament is not a book of theology here or anywhere else; but it can be seen in the way in which it speaks to men and deals with them. Jesus talks with all kinds of folk: fishermen and peasants, army officers and grafting tax collectors, church leaders and heretical Samaritans, prostitutes, condemned criminals, and children at play. To him these all belong to God; he believes it possible for all these to know God and live with him as children. As for Paul, the high ideal of his chapter on love was presented to these same Corinthians as a standard of life.

We will not understand this Christian conception, this strange paradox of severe condemnation and high demand and expectation, except as we see it against the background of the Christian faith. Christianity sees not just the man that is, but the man that may be, and not man by himself but man in relation to God. It judges so severely precisely because it holds this high ideal; it hopes so greatly because of its faith in God. Man is from God, man is made for God, and anything is possible for man through God. When, therefore, we are admonished to be realistic, and it is suggested that we move, with Reinhold Niebuhr, theologically right and economically left, we may agree provided we include the idealism of Christianity with its realism, and take care that we do not swing so far right with traditional theology as to move beyond both Jesus and Paul.

The old phrase from Genesis about man as made "in the image of God" will help to bring out the Christian point of view. Scholars are divided as to what the Genesis writer meant by these words, but the Christian meaning is not obscure. In a very real sense man is like God, and not all his evil can destroy this. He is person as God is, and not thing or beast. He belongs to the realm of the spirit, of love and truth and goodness; that is his glory if he rises to it; that is his greater condemnation if he falls. But this "image of God" points forward too; in its full sense it belongs to the future. It is not some past innocence of paradise, not some imagined perfection of being before the fall; it is the high end that is to be achieved. We are to be children of our Father in heaven, we are to grow up in him who is our head; "it doth not yet appear what we shall be," but we are to be like him.

QUESTIONS FOR DISCUSSION

In what ways has modern science helped us to a better understanding of human nature and how to deal with it?

At what points does man resemble the lower animals? At what points does he differ from them?

Compare the differing conceptions of human nature lying back of Fascism and democracy; of Calvinism and modern liberal thought in religion; of naturalism and idealism. Consider each position as to defects and elements of truth.

What are the important elements in the Christian conception of man? What significance do these have for our thought on social problems and our social theories?

FOR FURTHER READING

E. R. E.: Articles, "Soul," "Anthropology," "Evolution"
J. Y. Simpson: *Man and the Attainment of Immortality*
J. A. Thomson: *What Is Man?*
H. W. Robinson: *The Christian Doctrine of Man*
W. E. Hocking: *The Self, Its Body and Freedom*
G. H. Palmer: *The Problem of Freedom*
G. T. W. Patrick: *What Is the Mind?*
J. Laird: *The Idea of the Soul*
H. A. Overstreet: *A Book About Ourselves*
J. H. Coffin: *The Soul Comes Back*
W. Brown: *Science and Personality*

XI

WHAT SIN IS AND DOES

I. OUR LESSENED SENSE OF SIN

EVEN in religious circles one does not hear very much talk about sin today, and there is certainly everywhere a lessened sense of sin. Some of the change is to the good, for not a little of the old sense of sin was morbid and self-centered. It was not so much contrition for an evil life as it was fear of consequences, of judgment and hell; and often the men who talked most about sin had little concern for evils about them that called loudly for remedy. They were concerned about sin in the abstract, not about sins in the concrete. There has been, indeed, a deepening sense of the sins of the group, the wrongs for which the social body is to blame. Such evils as slavery and war lived on for centuries with little protest and little sense of guilt on the part even of Christian men. Walter Rauschenbusch tells the story of a farmer who was arrested and fined for selling dirty milk. His coreligionists disciplined him, not for his unsocial practice by which he had endangered the lives of babies, but because in anger at his arrest he had let loose a "damn." Today there is a growing social sense of sin; more and more people are seeing that war and racial hate and unemployment and poverty are sins for which we are responsible and of which we must repent.

But the loss of the sense of personal sin is another

matter, and it is not an advance. Whether we like this talk about sin or not, sin is a big fact in the world. The stories about it cover the front pages of our papers. The government recognizes its presence with police and courts and jails, and pays a crime bill that runs into billions. Our oppressive war costs are chargeable to the expense account of sin. And every last man of us knows it in his individual life. The right and good speak to me and I refuse them; that is sin. In my inner self there is a dualism, a lower self standing against the higher; that is sin. I turn to the good and something within me hinders me; that is sin.

Why is there a lessened sense of sin? There are two main reasons. One is a growing individualism which recognizes no authority, which knows no rule of life except its own interest and desire, which acknowledges no obligation except to itself. James Oppenheim has voiced this modern temper:

> "Let nothing bind you;
> If it is Duty, away with it.
> If it is Law, disobey it.
> If it is Opinion, go against it.
> There is only one Divinity, Yourself;
> Only one God, YOU."

It is not usually so frank as this. It talks about self-expression, but it fails to see that every man is two selves, and that this very fact brings us under the law of obligation. Modern individualism is a denial of the moral order; back of it is the loss of the moral sense.

The second reason is the growing naturalism, or secularism, which means the loss of the sense of God and spiritual reality. It is the lusty paganism seen in Walt Whitman's "Song of Myself."

"I think I could turn and live with the animals, they are
   so placid and self-contained;
 I stand and look at them long and long.
 They do not sweat and whine about their condition;
 They do not lie awake in the dark and weep for their
   sins;
 They do not make me sick discussing their duty to God."

If you live in a world of two dimensions, on the plane of things and in the world of now, you will not, of course, worry about your sins or think about God. But neither will you dream dreams or have hopes of better things to be. There will be no high goal to command you, no vision to inspire you, no faith in God to give courage to fight on. It is this same naturalism, this loss of faith in a God and a goal that give life meaning and hope, that has brought on the sense of futility and hopelessness which curses our age. Our age may sink to despair, or once more rise to faith and to the struggle for which it calls, but it cannot go back to care-free paganism. Such a paganism, a happy animalism, never, in fact, existed. For men have always been ruled either by faith or fear. In the old paganism it was fear, fear of unknown but dread spirits on every hand, fear of the incalculable forces of nature, fear of a grave that held no hope. And for the modern man it is the fear of a life that has no meaning, of a future without hope, of a universe of blind forces that will engulf us all at last, yes, and that fear of each other that is driving nations into the race of armaments whose burdens are breaking the back of toil.

The Christian doctrine of sin has two sides. On the

one it is a courageous facing of facts, without which
there can be no cure of our ills, individual or social.
Correct diagnosis must come before remedy. There
has been a kind of liberalism in religion and politics
which has seemed to think that all we needed to do
was to hold up an ideal and map out a program, and
the end was secured. Adopt a constitution and you
had a democracy; pass a prohibitory law and you had
a sober nation; establish a League of Nations and
you had world peace. It left out of account man and
sin; it shut its eyes to human ignorance and stupidity,
to selfishness and greed, to the fires of hate and anger
always smoldering just below the surface. Today
men are growing more "realistic," and everywhere
they see that first of all we must take human nature
into account.

But there is a second side to Christian teaching,
and that is one of hope. The fact is, Christianity
does not ask men to "whine about their condition,"
or "lie awake and weep for their sins." Christianity
believes in God and in the man that is to be. Its doctrine of sin is not one of pessimism or despair. It
faces the fact of sin and hauls it out into the light in
order that men may move beyond sin, that they may
put it behind them, set their face to the future, and
fix their faith in God. It speaks three words: good
news, repent, believe. In the word with which Jesus
began his work: "The Kingdom of God is at hand;
repent and believe the good news."

II. WHAT IS SIN?

Sin is evil in man seen in the light of God. **Three
considerations will bring out its meaning.**

1. Sin is the refusal of good; it is man's "No!" to the highest. We saw man's distinctive nature in the fact that he lives in two worlds, the actual and the possible, the "is" and the "ought to be." Animals may be ferocious, cruel, bloodthirsty; they are not sinful. They have no higher level to which to rise and so cannot fall to the lower. It is here that glory and tragedy lie side by side for man. The higher world comes with its invitation and demand. It brings what we know is just and right and good, with which we must square our lives. Our common speech reveals this; the good man is one who is square, straight, upright, on the level—all figures of speech which mean that he comes up to a certain standard. This is not a matter of rules to be followed; it is our higher self waiting to be achieved. It is beauty, truth, faith, love, joy, peace. It is life in the rich relations of home, friendship, community, nation, God, the life in which give and receive are inseparably joined. The chance to rise is the glory of man.

But man can refuse to grow. He can say "No" to life. Sin is this refusal. It is, first, disloyalty to ourselves. My true self, the real man, is not the "is," but that which "is to be"; and I can refuse that. As Gilbert Chesterton once suggested: You don't pat a crocodile on the back and say: "Now, be a crocodile." A crocodile cannot do anything else. But you do put your hand on a man's shoulder and say, "Now, be a man," for he may be a man, or he may not. Further, sin is disloyalty to my fellow men. For this higher that is to be is not an individual affair; it is a common life, a common good that calls, and it demands a common faith and devotion. Sin is the betrayal of my fellow man. And, finally, it is disloyalty to God, the refusal of his will and purpose, of life in fellowship in him.

That does not mean that there comes some dramatic moment in each life when we realize all this and make final choice of evil instead of good, pausing at our Rubicon and then deliberately crossing over. More often it is indifference, inertia, an aimless drifting with the current of ease and pleasure. But this, too, is disloyalty. Here is the place where neutrality is iniquity, or, rather, where there can be no neutrality. "He that is not for us is against us." This sin of negation is no little matter. It is not the calculating opposition of the wicked few but the selfish indifference of the many that has always been the real obstacle in the path of the kingdom of God. The most tragic feature in the scene at the cross was not the satisfaction of the few leaders who had achieved their vindictive end, nor the callous soldiers doing their appointed task, but the crowd who simply "stood beholding." It is because of just such a refusal that Browning passes his judgment on "The Lost Leader":

"Blot out his name, then, record one lost soul more,
　　One task more declined, one more footpath untrod,
One more devils' triumph and sorrow for angels,
　　One wrong more to man, one more insult to God!"

2. Sin is selfishness. Goodness and sin, in the last analysis, are not so much a matter of outward conduct or particular choices, but rather an inner spirit or attitude. Probably no single word will do, but if we chose one word for goodness it would be good will, or love, and for sin selfishness. Selfishness is

what lies behind disobedience, or disloyalty. We refuse God and the common good and the higher self because we prefer our own will and way. That is plain in the black sins of envy, deceit, hatred, greed, cruelty, lust, and murder; but the same principle is at work in the sins of mere inertia and indifference. Men do not choose evil because it is evil. When we find a man who deliberately seeks to inflict suffering on others for its own sake, we call him a monster, or we recognize with modern psychology that he is abnormal, not sane. What men are after in their sin is some sort of good or pleasure or satisfaction; but they seek it selfishly, putting the lower as against the higher, taking individual pleasure as supreme against God. They are like those "wretched souls," those evil angels whom Dante found shut out from heaven and denied admission even to hell,

> ". . . who nor rebellious proved
> Nor yet were true to God, but for themselves
> Were only."

3. Sin is wrongdoing seen in relation to God. Here religion adds its third dimension to the concept of sin and reveals its deepest meaning. Sin is something moral, the doing of wrong, the failure of right, but it is more; it is all this as seen in the light of God, and thus seen in its full meaning. If we are to understand this, we must first rid ourselves of the picture of God as a jealous Ruler sitting aloft and demanding his dues and honors, and of sin as the refusal which he punishes. Rather, God is he in whom all good has its being and source. Justice and love and truth are not abstractions; they live in God and God comes to us in them. In him are all the

high possibilities of life to which we are to give ourselves. To him, therefore, we are to bring all hope and trust, all aspiration and devotion. His will is our life, our good, our goal. Sin, then, is not merely this evil choice or that refusal; it is the denial of God and of his high purpose for man. Only faith in God can give to life its full meaning and glory; and only in the light of that faith do we see what sin really means. In that sense we say: "Against thee, thee only, have I sinned, and done that which is evil in thy sight." It is Isaiah's vision of God which causes him to cry out: "I am a man of unclean lips, and I dwell in the midst of a people of unclean lips." It is no morbid dwelling on man and his evil which brings Christianity's keen sense of sin; it is rather its high conception of a merciful and holy God and its lofty ideal for man.

III. The Consequences of Sin

One of the results of modern science has been to make men conscious of an all-embracing order within which all happenings in nature take place. There is no chance, nothing haphazard in the universe. It means tragic consequences sometimes, usually because of human ignorance or wilfulness; but it means a world in which science and control of nature and growing human welfare are possible, since nature is orderly and trustworthy. It is curious that men have been so slow to recognize a like order in the moral universe and to appreciate its value. Without such a moral order there could be no sure building up of character in the individual or of a just and stable social structure. But that same order means that corresponding consequences follow upon wrongdoing. Men have not seen this because they thought of the consequences of sin in terms of punishment, and punishment they conceived after the human manner as something imposed from without. Then they sentimentalized their idea of God, and insisted that he was too "good" to inflict pain on his children. From that fool's paradise we are awakening today to the stark fact that sin is real, that its consequences are destruction, and that they follow as the night the day.

Let us begin, then, not with the idea of punishment, but with that of a moral order in which human life is lived. Because sin is negative, the denial of the good, we can best understand it by asking what good is. The good that we seek is life, not just existence but life at its fullest and best; and life is a matter of right relations. Every step forward in the evolution of life upon earth was an entrance into larger relations. For no being do so many and such varied and meaningful relations wait as for man. The doors that open into this richer life are three: truth, or insight into what our world means and holds; obedience, or loyalty to the demand that these relations make upon us; and love, the willingness to forsake the narrow and selfish life and give ourselves to the larger life to which we may belong, to home, friend, country, humanity, God.

Sin is disloyalty and selfishness, and these bar the road of life. Sin is the refusal of obedience, of self-surrender, of love, of the high and adventurous quest. But always it is that which divides and so disintegrates and destroys. The reason we do not see this more clearly is because we do not see sin carried to its full consequences; but the word of James remains true: "Sin, when it is fullgrown, bringeth forth death."

The examples of all this are as varied as life. They appear in the physical realm. Not only do the vices of the flesh affect the body, but where anger, jealousy, hatred, and fear rule, there we find anarchy in the kingdom of the soul, there body and mind both suffer. Sin is divisive and disintegrative in social relations as well as in the individual. It separates man from man, and destroys that rich life which is found in human association. Back of war, of poverty, of political corruption, of scourges like typhoid, tuberculosis, and venereal disease, back of our varied social ills, are to be found greed and pride and lust for power and selfish indifference to others; in a word, back of them all is sin. How plain it is when we make an honest study of such an enemy to man as war is! This is what sin means and does when it has a chance in human life.

The deepest consequences of sin are seen in man's inner life. God is the source of our life; in its refusal, in its selfishness, sin means isolation and so, once more, death. The very selfishness which grasps at life is a refusal of life. As Browning says in "A Death in the Desert":

"This is death and the sole death,
When a man's loss comes to him from his gain,
Darkness from light, from knowledge ignorance,
A lamp's death when, replete with oil, it chokes."

Of all the consequences of sin the most tragic is sin itself. Man gets what he chooses. He turns from light, and the light that is in him becomes darkness. He refuses love, and isolation, emptiness, and loneliness are his lot. He says "No" to God, and God becomes ever less real while he loses the peace and courage and hope which have their source in him. From among his possible selves he chooses the lower and baser, and one day he realizes, as Stevenson has portrayed it in his drama of the soul, that Doctor Jekyll is gone and only the sinister, evil Mr. Hyde is left. The nations of the earth, careless of justice, indifferent to obligation, turning from co-operation to rivalry, from common good to selfish interest, relying on force of arms, obtain the judgment on their sins by receiving what they desire: a world of mingled hate and fear and war that threatens to engulf all in a common doom. Here, as Browning points out in his "Easter Day," following the word of Revelation 22. 11, is the hell that is God's punishment for sin:

> "Let such men rest
> Content with what they judged the best.
> Let the unjust usurp at will:
> The filthy shall be filthy still:
> Miser, there waits the gold for thee!
> Hater, indulge thine enmity!"

So sin is failure, salvation is life. Life is not easy; "I find it hard to be a Christian," writes Browning in this same poem. Jesus made that plain: the lamp must be lit, the loins girded about, we must sell all for the sake of the one pearl, of the treasure in the field. And when the hand is once on the plow, we must not look back. Sin means losing out. It may mean the refusal to surrender, or the choice of a lesser good, or failure in devotion and persistence. Its root may be folly or wilfulness or wickedness; but in any case it means losing the road, missing the mark, the failure to find life.

QUESTIONS FOR DISCUSSION

Compare the religious concept of sin with the ethical concept of the morally wrong. How does religion deepen the ethical concept?

Conceiving sin as essentially disloyalty and selfishness, consider the social significance of these as the underlying evil attitudes in the fields of industry, politics, and international relations. Give illustrations to support your position.

Do we need a deeper sense of sin? Have we more or less of this than our fathers? How could this be secured? Are there dangers here?

What is the effect of modern psychology on the idea of sin?

List in order what you consider the most serious sins in individual life. In society.

Does faith in a moral order involve belief in the punishment of sin? Consider right and wrong conceptions of such punishment.

FOR FURTHER READING

R. S. Moxon: *The Doctrine of Sin*
C. E. Barbour: *Sin and the New Psychology*
E. A. Ross: *Sin and Society*
Walter Rauschenbusch: *A Theology for the Social Gospel*
W. Cosby Bell: *The Making of Man*
W. M. Horton: *A Psychological Approach to Theology*
E. R. E.: and Hastings' *D. B.*: Article, "Sin"
F. R. Tennant: *The Concept of Sin*
Consult also works on theology by Knudson, Clarke, and Brown listed in Chap. I.

XII

WHAT DOES IT MEAN TO BE SAVED?

I. The Place of Salvation in Religion

Religion has three aspects: it is a faith that we hold, a life that we live, a help that we receive. Salvation means religion as a way of help. There are some who feel that this side of religion belongs to the past. Not as much is said about salvation in the Church as there once was. There are various reasons for this. (1) Men found the old ideas of salvation no longer convincing or adequate. The old preaching was individual; it had no word for the great social needs. It was otherworldly; it did not enough realize that religion must bring life here and now. It was narrow, concerned mainly with escape from punishment for sin, or absorbed in some "scheme" of atonement or plan of salvation by which a man could be forgiven and get to heaven. (2) Men became more concerned in the human side of religion, in what man himself could and should do. (3) With the coming of science and modern inventions, the age of machinery and of multiplied wealth and comforts, men grew more interested in material goods and more confident that they could solve their own problems. (4) As the physical world grew in meaning and attractiveness, men lost their interest in spiritual values; the sense of the reality of God and of man's dependence on him weakened, and secularism and paganism increased. Within the Church itself, with the growth of organ-

167

ization and activity, there was a decreased sense of God as a power in men's lives.

But the movement has not all been one way. The situation has been changing rapidly since the first decade of our century. (1) There is a new realism today that has taken the place of the old optimism and romanticism. We see more clearly the forces of evil in our social order. We know how long and hard the fight is going to be if truth and justice and peace are to win out. We realize the darker passions and evil forces in human nature; the World War showed us how thin was the veneer of "culture," how near the surface everywhere was the old savagery. Men are talking of impending doom, of the race between education and destruction. (2) Increasing numbers are coming to see where our problem lies and what the help must be. Science and invention will not save us, for we have seen their use as instruments of destruction. World Courts and Peace Pacts and League of Nations cannot deliver us, nor political and economic reform. All have their place but all are useless unless there comes also a radical change in the spirit of men. Many have repeated with Sir Philip Gibbs, the great war correspondent, "Europe needs a new heart;" and so do Asia and America. (3) The modern man, throwing aside the old beliefs and authorities, is as deeply in need of help as ever his father was. Freed from the old restraints, as Walter Lippmann has pointed out, he does not know where to go or what to do with his life. Life has lost meaning because he has lost God. The boom days leave him restless and dissatisfied; depression days find him helpless and hopeless. (4) So far from the idea of salvation dropping out, our race has never seen a day when men in their need listened to so many voices promising deliverance. Communism and Fascism are the new messiahs hailed by vast populations, while endless panaceas are heralded in other lands. Meanwhile multitudes turn to the many cults that offer salvation, to theosophy, Christian Science, spiritualism, healing missions, millennial movements, or to the psychoanalyst.

The idea of salvation has a clear and permanent place. All life has two sides, the active and the receptive. Salvation deals with the second side, that of our dependence, or need of help. Physically we are dependent every moment upon what the world gives us of light, air, and food. Socially we are helpless if left to ourselves. Salvation represents this dependence and help on the highest level. Back of it lies a threefold conviction: there are evils from which we need deliverance; there is a good for us to attain; there is a world of spiritual being and power from which we may have help. The last point is the crux of the matter. We know the world of physical forces; we see clearly that human life and progress have depended upon man's understanding those forces, and relating himself rightly to them. But we have not known how to use the spiritual forces of life. Outward wealth and inner bankruptcy have gone together; and unless we can gain inner resources and strength, it is clear that scientific knowledge and material wealth will avail us nothing. But just as electricity long waited for us to know it and use it in transforming the earth, so there are spiritual forces waiting for man's understanding and use. There is peace for our unrest, forgiveness for our sin, strength in place of our moral impotence, healing for our social strife and inner discords, and hope that can look death, the inevitable, in the face.

In its full scope, the idea of salvation includes three aspects: the problem of the individual, the making of a new social order, and the life beyond. This chapter deals with the individual.

II. To What Are We Saved?

To understand what salvation means we must ask three questions: To what? From what? By what? To what are we to be saved? Webster says salvation is "preservation from destruction or calamity; deliverance from sin and its consequences." But it is more than that. It is something positive, the good that we desire. Is that good happiness, success, power, personal development, heaven? There is but one adequate word and that is "life." Salvation means to gain life, life at its fullest and highest. In Tennyson's word,

> " 'Tis life whereof our nerves are scant,
>   O life, not death, for which we pant ;
>   More life and fuller that I want."

"Life" is one of those words, like "truth" and "beauty" and "right," which you cannot define because it is unique and ultimate. We can, however, say some things about life that will help show what it means. Life is a matter of relations. We may smile at the tautology of Webster's definition, that life is the "fact of being alive," but the phrase is significant. Life is more than existence. The meaning of life and its measure are to be found in the range of things to which we are alive and the degree of our aliveness. The simplest plant is alive to sun and rain, to earth and air. The dog has a far more varied and interesting world—think of a dog in the country on a fresh summer morning, alive to his master and to all the scents and sounds of field and wood. Man is the creature who belongs to the greatest variety of worlds and is alive to them in the most intense and meaningful manner. That is what makes a man's life. He is a physical being, with an interest in food, drink, pain, pleasure, work, rest, and other bodily concerns. He is a social being, entering into the myriad relations with his fellows in home and society which give his life such varied and engrossing interests. He is a personal being, not only conscious like the dog but self-conscious, with an inner world of his own. Beauty speaks to him in color, form, and sound; the majestic and sublime enthrall him; truth summons him to endless search; the stern yet appealing realities of the moral order, of all that is just and good, lay hold upon him. And in his times of clearest vision he knows that he belongs to the world of the Eternal, to the life of fellowship with God. This is what life means, not just existence, but to be alive to all these worlds and to all that they offer.

The story of the development of life on earth will help us to understand this. In a fascinating philosophical work, *Holism and Evolution* ("holism" is from a Greek word meaning "whole"), Jan Smuts has described the process of evolution as one of the making of wholes. The electric particles unite to form the atom, the atoms unite in molecules of different character, the building-blocks out of which our physical world is made. The living cell marks another and far richer "whole," and begins another movement of advance. But at every stage the process follows a common principle: the individual or particular is summoned to unite with a larger whole and so to rise in the scale of life. So hydrogen and oxygen unite to form water, that compound which is as essential to life as it is indispensable to the beauty of nature, which transcends anything that we can find in oxygen or hydrogen taken alone. So the particles which form the living cell share in a life far beyond anything that might come to them apart from this new relation. The law of life in its advance is the same: find a greater world, a richer whole; give yourself to it, lose yourself in it, in order that you may find yourself again in a fuller measure of life. The mark of man above all other animals is to be found in those many wholes, those relations of life, or worlds of being, to which he can thus give himself. The goal of creation on earth seems to be this creature, man, with body, mind, imagination, affections, spirit, will, who can see these many worlds and enter into living relations with them.

Salvation, then, means the gaining of life, life at its richest and fullest, a life that is given to us as we enter into right relations with that world on which we depend. It does not have to do with a segment of life that we call spiritual, or with saving some inner core or part of our nature which we call soul. It is the man's whole being that is to be redeemed, indeed, his whole world. It is a mark of that development noted above, in which life moves from lower levels to higher, that the lower is never lost as life moves up. The lower becomes the foundation of the higher and is taken up in it. The healthy body is a necessary condition of the life of the spirit, at the same time contributing to that life joys of its own. The mind, trained, alert, clear-thinking, renders high service and brings its own rich gifts. And so we move up into the ethical, the social, and finally into fellowship with God.

Four main relations constitute the sphere of man's life: nature, self, man's fellows, and God. Religion includes all and emphasizes the last, but the relation with God is not just a fourth added to the other three. We might call each of these relations a dimension of life. As each higher dimension comes it does not simply add; it transforms the whole. So the supreme relation, God, the last dimension of life, the Eternal, transforms all the rest as it takes them up into itself. He who finds God learns for the first time what the world and his brother and his own life mean; through God alone these come to their full meaning and expression. He learns how to enjoy this world without becoming its slave, to rule it instead of being its servant, to dwell in it without fear. And he learns how to live with his brother. Here, then, is the supreme matter in salvation, to come into right relation with God and so through him to find all else.

The question is often raised in religion as in education, Is the final end self-realization or service? Or were the fathers right when they said it was to glorify God? But these ends are not opposed or exclusive. On the contrary, each involves the others. Religion is more than self-realization, or culture; it is finding the Highest and giving yourself in reverence and devotion, forgetting yourself because you have found something infinitely greater than yourself. Nor will you ever find yourself until you have thus found something higher—"He that will save his life shall lose it." And that applies to God and the service of my fellows. But the service of God is not a thing apart; we serve him as we serve them—"Inasmuch as ye did it unto one of these my brethren, ye did it unto me." But if God and my brother belong here, my own life is not left out. My own personality is one of God's ends; that, too, is sacred. Jesus' word was not, "Thou shalt love thy neighbor and not thyself," but, "Thou shall love thy neighbor as thyself."

III. From What Are We Saved?

Life, we have seen, means the fullest attainment of our possibilities through right relations with God and our world. We need to be saved from all that stands in its way.

1. There are physical conditions: poverty, sickness, economic uncertainty, suffering, death. Religion is not without concern for these, but they are not our immediate problem.

2. Fear is one of the greatest threats to peace and strength of life. Social and psychological study has made that increasingly plain. There is fear of the world in which we live, of blind forces that seem to hold us, of the uncertain future, of inevitable death. There is fear of men, of what men think of us, of what they may do. And there is fear of ourselves: doubt, distrust, the sense of inferiority, crippling and

often destroying. Fear means darkness, suffering, and the paralysis of life's energies.

3. We need deliverance from the sense of futility, the feeling of the aimlessness and meaninglessness of life which has made such deep inroads on the modern spirit. "The modern man," writes Walter Lippmann, "who has ceased to believe without ceasing to be credulous, hangs, as it were, between heaven and earth, and is at rest nowhere. There is no theory of the meaning and value of events which he is compelled to accept, . . . no inevitable purpose in the universe." A famous caricaturist, brilliantly successful, left a revealing note after committing suicide: "I have had few real difficulties," he wrote; "on the contrary, an exceptionally glamorous life, as life goes, and more than my share of affection and appreciation. . . . I am fed up with inventing devices for getting through twenty-four hours every day. . . . I have run from wife to wife, from house to house, and from country to country in a ridiculous effort to escape myself." We need deliverance because we have lost God who is the meaning and goal of life.

4. We need deliverance from ignorance. There is not only folly, whose eyes are closed to life's real goods, but there is ignorance of the waiting forces with which our world is filled, the resources of help and strength. We are like the natives who once roamed over this land, who hungered though treading the most fertile soil of earth, who froze when beneath them were waiting beds of coal, who bent their backs to heavy burdens when in the earth and in flowing water there was unused power to do all their work. Ignorance is keeping us from the life

that would come if we knew how to relate ourselves to the spiritual forces of the universe.

5. We need to be saved from ourselves. We are getting past the superficial romanticism and smug complacency which supposed that man was all right though society or the world was wrong, that we all were inherently good and only needed a fair chance, that self-expression was our supreme right and our only need. What if we haven't the right kind of self to express? Or what if we are many selves and not one? What if the wrong self has been coming out on top, and, more and more, with its selfishness, lust, greed, fear, and vanity, has been establishing itself as the only self? What if, like Paul and many another, I see the better and approve it, and choose the worse? "Who will rescue me from this body of death?"

6. That means that I need to be saved from my past, from the consequences of what I have done, and what I deserve. There is, of course, a law of consequences as inevitable in the spiritual world as in the natural. Some of these consequences remain unalterable. But there are consequences that can be overcome when new and higher forces enter in, or when man is set into new relations. My ignorance and selfishness and sin have destroyed the right relations of life. They have set me against God, against my fellows; they have put me out of harmony with the world of nature, and made me a divided self. From these destroyed fellowships and wrong relations I must and can be saved.

And now we can see more clearly what being lost and being saved mean. We are lost when we are out of place, out of right relations, on the wrong road. It is not destruction. Among the thousand papers in my filing cabinet there is one that is lost. I know it is there, somewhere; but it is lost because it is out of place. We are lost when we are cut off from God, from our fellows, from the true task of life, when we are severed from these by ignorance and selfishness, by lack of faith and loyalty and good will. To be saved means somehow to be set into right relations. That means life, and only so can life come.

IV. BY WHAT ARE WE SAVED?

1. It is interesting to note some of the ways by which men have sought salvation. (1) Magic is the crudest of these. It is the dependence on rites and incantations, on signs and lucky objects. Science shows its futility. Religion condemns it because its whole spirit and attitude are wrong; for it seeks to master and compel the unseen forces for its selfish ends, whereas religion calls for humble and reverent devotion. Yet there are great numbers still who mix magic with their religion or make it a substitute. (2) Ritual and offering and sacrament are everywhere a form of religious life. As symbols to set forth the unseen, and as ways of expressing devotion and entering into communion with God, they are of real help. But when a church says, "God has prescribed these particular forms and ways; apart from these there is no salvation, and he has committed these to us alone," then they do not represent truly either God or the way of life. And when men think that consecrated water placed on an infant, or consecrated bread taken by an adult, somehow trans-

forms the essence or nature of the human soul with a kind of mechanical inevitability, then we must find in this a survival of magic. (3) Asceticism is an ancient way, surviving here and there, though the spirit of our age is all against it. For it the material and natural as such are evil; and he who would find God and the spiritual must renounce and flee the world and the flesh. (4) Very old is the idea of salvation by "gnosis," which literally means "knowledge." In its broadest form it stands for the opinion that suffering is due to ignorance, our failures to lack of knowledge, that science is our messiah, that to know the good is to do it. But often it takes the form of systems like theosophy or Christian Science, offering men some special revealed insight, declaring that he who sees this and holds it is redeemed from all error, mortality, and suffering, and lifted to light and life.

Excepting magic only, there is something of truth in all these ways. But, aside from their errors, they do not get at the heart of the matter. Three facts must first be recognized. (1) Salvation is a personal and ethical affair. No man is saved until he is himself made over, until he is a new man, at one with himself where once he was divided, confident where he was anxious and fearful, master where once he was limited and bound, delivered from futility and aimlessness because he has found a high and satisfying goal, and fundamentally right within because of a new spirit of love and truth. (2) A man can be so changed only as he is brought into right relations, first with God in whom is all truth and life, then, and through this, with all his world.

2. There are many today who would rule out the idea of salvation altogether. Man needs saving, they say, but he must save himself; we must not expect any Power to reach down from the skies and help us. That was natural enough, they declare, in a day when men stood helpless before famine and storm and pestilence, and cried out in despair for aid; now it means laziness or superstition. The means of help are in our own hands and there is no other. Our science enables us to use the forces of nature. Our social problems will be settled when we learn to work together through economics, politics, diplomacy, and education. And for our personal problems we have the new psychology. If we are behaviorists, we will plan to "condition" or "recondition" man by properly controlled and applied stimuli, beginning, of course, with infancy, until we have made man just what he should be. If we are Freudians, we have the instruments of analysis and therapy by which to bring to light the hidden sources of frustration and fear, make whole the divided soul, and make it happy by setting it into right social relations. Such is the general position of naturalistic humanism.

There is some truth here that we must recognize. No community has the right to expect God to stop a typhoid epidemic because people pray for it; it will cease when the milk and water supply is kept pure, and when the city government is cleaned up whose inefficiency and corruption have made such conditions possible. No man can expect to be made over into a strong, well-poised character by simply folding his hands and asking God to do it; salvation is not "direct action" by divine power, as bricks are made

by a mold. But this does not answer the question;
it simply helps to correct misunderstandings. What
has religion to say?

3. First, religion declares that there is a spiritual environment that is more real, more intimate,
more powerful than our physical surroundings, the
God upon whom we depend more immediately and
absolutely than we do on light and air and food. The
meaning of this God for our life cannot be put in a
word. (1) He is sustaining Energy, in whom electrons and stars and men all "live and move and have
their being." (2) He is the Order which at once sets
limits to our action and makes our life possible. (3)
He is the Purpose that is achieving itself in the universe through the ages. (4) But more than all this,
God is Person, calling us to enter into fellowship, to
link our life to his in understanding and faith and
loyalty; he is Love that forgives our sins and shares
with us its life.

Second, religion declares that there are laws in
this world of the spirit, that there are ways by which
we may find God and gain life through fellowship
with him. This important practical question will
concern us in the next two chapters.

Questions for Discussion

What is the meaning of salvation and the place of this
idea in religion?

Is there a lessened interest in this idea today in the
churches and outside? If so, why?

What are some of the modern ways in which this interest
is expressing itself outside of the churches?

What are the evils from which man needs to be saved?

Consider the changing conceptions in religion and elsewhere as to the supreme goods which men are seeking.

Consider the following as ways in which men are seeking salvation today: prayer, the sacraments, mysticism, social reform or revolution, Christian Science, the new psychology (psychoanalysis, psychotherapy), theosophy. Add to the list. Note the elements of truth and error, strength and limitation in all of these.

FOR FURTHER READING

W. Cosby Bell: *The Making of Man*

W. E. Hocking: *Man and His Remaking*

L. D. Weatherhead: *Psychology in Service of the Soul*

J. G. Mackenzie: *Souls in the Making*

E. M. Ligon: *The Psychology of Christian Personality*

A. C. Underwood: *Conversion, Christian and Non-Christian*

H. N. and R. W. Wieman: *Normative Psychology of Religion*

E. S. Waterhouse: *What Is Salvation?*

J. B. Pratt: *The Religious Consciousness,* Chaps. VII to IX

XIII

SALVATION: THE CHRISTIAN WAY

OUR study has made plain that the final answer to man's problem must be both radical and inclusive. It must be radical in getting at the root of the trouble within man himself and finding a way by which this man can be made over. It must be inclusive in giving meaning to his world and in relating him rightly to this whole world: to nature, to fellow man, and to God. What, now, has Christianity to offer?

I. GOD AS THE CHALLENGE TO MAN

Jesus' first word when he began preaching was not "man" but "God." "The rule of God is at hand; repent and believe the good news." It is interesting to hear the word of the new psychology as represented by C. G. Jung in his volume, *Modern Man in Search of a Soul.* "During the past thirty years people from all the civilized countries of the earth have consulted me. Among all my patients in the second half of life, that is to say, over thirty-five, there has not been one whose problem in the last resort was not that of finding a religious outlook on life." The real cause of the patient's illness, he declares, "arises from his having no love, but only sexuality; no faith, because he is afraid to grope in the dark; no hope, because he is disillusioned by the world and life; and no understanding, because he has failed to read the meaning of his own experience." Neuroses grow as religious faith declines. "What the patient needs in order to live," he says, "is faith, hope, love, and insight" (pp. 260, 264). This is Hocking's idea of a revolution through a "radical insight," and God is that insight. It is this challenge of God with which Christianity confronts man, declaring that only so can he see himself and his world and find life. How, then, does God challenge man?

1. There is the challenge of goodness. God is the pure spirit of truth and love and righteousness. Christianity sees that spirit of God in the spirit of Jesus Christ. This is the vision that is at once the glory, the despair, and the hope of humanity. (1) Here is the glory of man. It sets him apart from all his fellow creatures. It shows him where his true life lies, what he may be, what he must be. It is an appeal to achievement and a command to obedience which we cannot escape. (2) Here is our judgment and our despair. We can be fairly complacent when we look at our fellow men. They are, after all, not so different from ourselves, nor can they see us as we really are; so we rationalize our conduct and save our self-esteem. But here is a light that searches our soul and reveals depths of evil which we did not suspect. Before this holiness and love we stand condemned. (3) In this goodness is the hope of man. For the goodness of God is mercy. That was the never-failing theme with Jesus and Paul: the goodness of God does not simply call for obedience and condemn failure; it is forgiving, redemptive, creative.

2. To believe in God means to believe in a universe of purpose; it is a summons to confidence and courage, to loyalty and adventurous living. God has a purpose for this world that is being worked out

through the ages. Just as there is an order of cause in the world, so there is also an order of ends; to believe in God is to believe in this order of ends. Evil is real but it is not final; there is a coming rule of justice and love, and the power of the universe is behind this purpose. Here God confronts our fears and destroys them. Faith in God is redemption from fear. Our deepest interests are not at the mercy of chance and change and death.

> "I stand amid th' eternal ways,
> And what is mine shall seek my face."

Here is a challenge to that cynicism and world weariness, that sense of futility which comes to every age, as it has to ours, when it loses God, when its world becomes an empty shell or the tragic arena of blind forces in unmeaning conflict. But this idea of a divine purpose is not only a challenge to fear and futility; it confronts the will of man. It challenges purpose. It condemns the aimless and selfish life. It gives high meaning to life, but only as we bring supreme devotion. It calls for adventurous living as we commit ourselves to the high end.

3. God means available life and power for man; as such he is a challenge to our moral impotence, to the shallowness and weakness of our inner life. Our central problem, in last analysis, is that of inner resources; it is one of dynamic. To believe in God is to believe that there are resources available for the spirit of man, just as truly as there is power to propel our machines, to light our streets, to warm our homes, and to supply our bodies with energy. Christianity offers a way to such resources.

II. The Response of Man to God

"God" is the first word and the last word in the Christian hope, but he is not the only word. Religion means relation; there is no religion until man makes answer to God. The two errors which threaten religion today are humanism and absolutism. The former rules out God and makes man not only central but self-sufficient, with nature as his servant. The latter makes God so absolute, so dominant, that time and earth lose all meaning and value, and man becomes a helpless pawn in the game that God plays. The effort to exalt and glorify God has resulted, not only in an unchristian conception of man, but in a less than Christian conception of God. For the Christian, God is not arbitrary will or irresistible force; he is Person speaking to person, love and truth claiming the understanding and free loyalty of man. Man must make answer to God; it takes two to make a relationship. What does Christianity say as to the human answer? What is the response demanded when such a God confronts us?

1. The first demand is for an inner revolution, an about-face in our inner spirit and attitude. If there is such a God, if this is what life means, then the old attitudes and old ways are wrong, and they must go. To find the wealth of life in things, to make the rule of life selfishness, to get money and power so that you can make others serve you, to rely upon force, to believe only in what you can see—this is the spirit that has usually ruled men and nations.

Now, until that spirit is radically changed, there is no hope for us individually or socially. This nation began its life in a revolution; we need some more revolutions today. Revolution does not as such imply violence; Webster defines it simply as radical, or fundamental change. Certainly, such change is needed in our social institutions—in industry, race relations, international relations, and political life. But these will avail little, they will not even be possible, except as we have an inner revolution as well. Carl Sandberg, in vernacular but with vigor, portrays the cynical, selfish spirit of the city.

> "Play it across the table.
> What if we steal this city blind?
> If they want anything, let 'em nail it down.

> "Harness bulls, dicks, front-office men,
> And the high goats up on the bench,
> Ain't they all in cahoots?
> Ain't it fifty-fifty all down the line?"

The language of diplomacy is different, but when we let the facts speak and see the motives that were really at work in the World War, the Versailles treaty, and the years of arming and scheming and fighting that have followed, we have the same selfishness, ruthlessness, hardness, and indifference to truth and justice. How can there be a new order without a new spirit?

So when Jesus held up God and his high purpose, and looked at the world of men's hearts, he cried out: "The rule of God is at hand; repent." The word "repentance" has lost much of its strength by narrow and petty usage. It has come to mean for many an emotional episode. The Greek word of our New Testament means literally a change in thought, or mind; it means an inner revolution, a revolution of mind and will and feeling. To see God means for us a reversal of values, a transformation of our hates and loves, an about-face of the will. It is no mere opinion. It means to see the evil for what it is, to hate it and turn from it, to turn with equal passion of devotion to the good, and so to re-orient our whole life. That is the first demand of Jesus.

2. The second demand is expressed in the word "faith." That too has suffered from narrow and false conceptions. Faith does not mean holding certain opinions, or submitting to some creed or authority in religion. Faith is a trust that rests on an inner conviction and issues in action. Faith like this, thoughtful but earnest, not credulous but with the courage to venture, ready to trust and act when once it meets that which deserves confidence and obedience—this is the absolute condition of all life and of the Christian life first of all. "The way to experience," writes C. G. Jung in the volume quoted above, "is a venture which requires us to commit ourselves with our whole being." It is quite literally true, as Mark 16. 16 reads in the old version: "He that believeth not shall be damned." Only, "damned" means something more than the medieval hell of flames; it is the loss of life.

The Christian challenge to faith is simple in meaning and searching in demand. Back of this universe there is a Love which offers us forgiveness and fellowship, a creative Good Will that is bringing in a kingdom of justice and mercy, a Power available for our lives. This God has spoken to men in Jesus Christ, in his word and life, in his love and death. Believe that, live in that faith; then life from God, life at its richest will be yours. Surely, it is plain that if there be such a God, faith is the one answer that is demanded; but it must be faith in this large sense, the response of the whole man, of mind and heart and will.

III. The Death of Christ and the Saving of Men

The Church of the past has always laid great stress upon the death of Christ in relation to human salvation. The teaching most commonly held was somewhat as follows: "Man has sinned against God and so is worthy of death. Christ took the place of man, dying in his stead. Thus the honor of God (or the demand of justice) is satisfied and man can be forgiven." The objections to this are obvious. It fails to see where the real problem of saving men lies. It is not a courtroom affair, a plan by which a debt can be paid or a penalty remitted. That really rules out the mercy of God, for when once a debt is paid there is no need of forgiveness and no place for it. Forgiveness is not a legal matter but one of moral-personal relations, and the problem lies in man and not in God. It is far more serious than the old teaching suggested. Here is man the sinner. His trouble is not simply his evil past; it is what he is now. He does not see the truth, he does not love the right things, he does not have God. What will bring this man into fellowship with God and make him over?

The modern man, however, priding himself on his breadth, may easily be narrower and more superficial here than the traditionalist. There is a double modern delusion. The first concerns the matter of forgiveness. Someone asked Heine, old and feeble, whether he did not fear death and what might follow. "Oh, no," he replied, "the good God will forgive. *C'est son métier*—That's his business." But forgiveness is not so simple. You cannot get rid of consequences in the moral world by just waving your hand. It is more than cancelling a debt; it is getting men into fellowship with God, into right relations in life, opening their eyes, getting them to hate evil and love the good and trust the Highest. The second delusion is the idea that when men once see the truth, the job is done. But the springs of life are not so easily touched. Men are not made over in their hates and loves and highest devotions simply by words or abstract ideas. Life is only changed by life.

It is not theory but a plain fact of history that Jesus was the beginning of a new spiritual epoch in human history, that he transformed a group of followers by his life and death, and that through the ages he has constantly released these spiritual forces among men. What does it mean when all these men tell us that it is the Christ of the cross that is the center of their faith? It does not mean that this particular instrument of a shameful death, this cross, has any particular significance, or that there is any special power in a man's dying. Many an innocent man endured this torture under Roman rule. But the Christ that has laid hold on men's faith and love is the Christ that died, the Man who was more than teacher, more than a noble example, who paid the last full measure of devotion in love to men and obedience to the will of God. And there is something still more important to see: it is not Christ that saves, it is God in Christ. What these men saw was that God had spoken, that God had come near. Here is the most daring belief that man ever ventured upon—to hold that the Eternal God was present in this life of a humble carpenter, in this love, in this suffering and death. So Alfred Noyes asks the question in "The Last Voyage":

> "Did his creation, then, involve descent,
> Renunciation, sacrifice in heaven,
> A Calvary at the inmost heart of things,
> Wherein an eternal passion still enacts
> In an eternal world what mortal eyes
> Saw dimly on one shadowy hill of time?"

Here is the profoundest meaning of the cross: the law of life is self-giving love, and such a love serves men by suffering in their stead. It is the law of God's life; it must become the law of man's life. For us, whose natural impulse is the selfish seeking of ease and avoidance of pain, that is a hard saying, but there are many witnesses to it. A distinguished Indian scholar, not a Christian himself, Professor Radakrishnan, writes in his volume, *East and West in Religion:* "The mystery of life is creative sacrifice. It is the central idea of the cross, which was such a scandal to the Jews and the Greeks, that he who truly loves us will have to suffer for us, even to the point of death. . . . The cross signifies that evil, in the hour of its supreme triumph, suffers its decisive defeat by the force of patient love and suffering. . . . The world belongs to the suffering rebels, the unarmed challengers of the mighty, the meek resisters who put truth above policy, humanity above country, love above force."

And now we can see some of the reasons for the potency in the remaking of men that has belonged to this Christ, who loved and lived and died in this way. We look at his death: Here is love at its high-est, God's love; here is revealed what sin actually is, sin that could do a deed like this. Black against white, evil against good, here they stand in eternal opposition. And they speak to us, as no mere words can, about God and life, about sin and the love that saves.

IV. The Remaking of Man

We are all agreed that salvation does not mean a mere escape from hell or getting to heaven, but that it means the making of men or, facing the fact of evil in men, their remaking. Can men be remade, and, if so, how?

Yes, says Christianity, men can be made over and have been without number. What is it that makes the real nature, or character, of a man? It is what he loves, what he hates, what he believes in, what he lives for. Find these and you find the real man. And all these can be radically changed. Sometimes this truth has been made difficult. It has been set forth as something wholly mysterious, if not magical. It has been limited to some great emotional experience or pictured as a sort of sudden transformation of soul substance. It has, indeed, been sudden and dra-matic at times, as when the light came to Paul on his way to Damascus, or when gay young Francis of Assisi one day turned his back on his home of wealth and life of pleasure, literally dropped his fine attire, and went forth naked to be "the little poor one," the brother of beggar and leper, of bird and beast. William James has given abundant illustration of this in his great work, *The Varieties of Religious Experience*. John Masefield has pictured it in his "Everlasting Mercy:"

> "I did not think, I did not strive,
> The deep peace burnt my me alive;
> The bolted door had broken in,
> I knew that I had done with sin.
> I knew that Christ had given me birth
> To brother all the souls of earth.
> And every bird and every beast
> Should share the crumbs broke at the feast."

Most often, however, the change is not sudden and dramatic. The essential fact is simply this, that men can be made over in their deepest nature by vital relation to the world of the spirit.

A popular word for this change today is integration. It is a most suggestive term. It means literally to unify, to make whole or complete. But what is often overlooked here is the fact that no man can be made whole without belonging to a whole. The process is this: find something higher and greater, give yourself to it, and in this larger whole find your true self and your richest life. Christianity declares that the highest that includes all is found when we find God. Integration is not enough; it must have the right center around which the integration takes place.

The common Christian word is the new birth, though the figure is older than Christianity. One birth is not enough for man; life is really a process of births. New Worlds come to us, rising one above the other—physical, mental, social, moral, aesthetic. To enter each, to rise to each level in turn as it summons us, is to find a richer life, to be born again. But the new birth that religion brings probes so deep, reaches so to the center, so includes all good, that we rightly keep this word for the change that it works. And the word well describes what Paul has in mind when he writes: "If any man is in Christ, he is a new creation." But it can be made simpler than all this if put in personal terms. God is our life. To find him, to give ourselves utterly to him, to love him and see all things in him and live in him—that is the life that is life indeed. Christ shows the way to that life. To accept him as Lord is to enter into that life. To enter it means to open the door to those forces which make life new and which make men over.

QUESTIONS FOR DISCUSSION

In what way is God a challenge to man?

What attitudes and acts on man's part are the fitting and necessary response to God?

Discuss the statement: The way of life (salvation) is integration through right relations. Give illustrations. Show the significance of the Christian way in this connection.

What forgiveness means and costs between man and man, and between God and man.

The meaning of the cross for us today in relation to God, to salvation, and to the life of men with each other.

The meaning of conversion and its place in salvation.

FOR FURTHER READING

The references in the last chapter should be consulted in connection with these.

G. W. Richards: *Christian Ways of Salvation*
E. R. E.: Articles, "Salvation," "Soteriology," "Faith"
G. B. Stevens: *The Christian Doctrine of Salvation*
George Cross: *The Christian Salvation*
John W. Oman: *Grace and Personality*
Philip Cabot: *Except Ye Be Born Again*

John Baillie: *The Place of Jesus Christ in Modern Christianity*
Edwin Lewis: *Jesus Christ and the Human Quest*
James Denney: *Jesus and the Gospel*
William James: *The Varieties of Religious Experience* (especially the sections on conversion)

XIV

THE WAYS OF LIFE

ROGER BABSON reports a visit that he once had with Charles P. Steinmetz, the world's outstanding electrical engineer of the last generation, in which they discussed the future of inventions. He put to Steinmetz the question: "What line of research will see the greatest development during the next fifty years?" And the answer came: "I think the greatest discovery will be made along spiritual lines. Here is a force which history clearly teaches has been the greatest power in the development of men and history. Yet we have merely been playing with it, and have never seriously studied it as we have the physical forces. Some day people will learn that material things do not bring happiness and are of little use in making men and women creative and powerful. Then the scientists of the world will turn their laboratories over to the study of God and prayer and spiritual forces. When this day comes, the world will see more advancement in one generation than it has seen in the past four." In these last four generations mankind has made incredible advances in the mastery of the physical world and the production of wealth. Just now it is facing the social-economic problem, the task of working out right relations between man and man, so that we shall not suffer from want in the midst of plenty, or destroy each other in war. But we cannot escape

the third question, which Steinmetz raises: How
shall we have wealth within? How shall we gain
for ourselves strength and poise and peace and joy
in life? For here is our worst failure. There is a
world of spiritual life and power just as real as the
physical world. Like the physical world it has its
laws, its order; and if we will adjust ourselves to it,
its resources may be ours.

At one point Steinmetz was wrong; we have much
to learn, but this world and its laws are not unknown. Many men have learned these laws, not in
the laboratories of science but in that of life, where
alone they can be discovered. They have found certain definite ways of life, simple but absolute, ways
to which man must conform if he would gain this
inner satisfaction and wealth. First among these
discoverers is Jesus. Some time ago the distinguished physicist and inventor, Michael Pupin, in a
volume called *The New Reformation* traced the steps
in the advance of physical science. Then, in his con-
cluding chapter, he turned to the spiritual realm.
As there have been master discoverers in thermo-
dynamics and electrodynamics, he declared, so in
spiritual dynamics Jesus stands forth as the supreme
discoverer of the laws of power.

Our task is to consider those ways which have been
found by men of insight and tested through the
years. Richard C. Cabot, distinguished writer in
medicine and ethics, filling chairs in both fields at
Harvard, wrote a book on *What Men Live By*. Work,
play, love, and worship are his four great words. He
began as a doctor concerned especially with neuras-
thenics; he became interested in that problem of the

inner life which underlies all the problems of health of mind and body. He came at last to see that educators, social workers, and physicians all agreed on one prescription, which he puts thus:

℞

REAL LIFE   an indefinite amount
Take a full dose after meals and at bedtime

That is the answer. The way to life is life—not to run away from life, not to devote yourself to a little section of life called spiritual, certainly not to live on unthinkingly or meanly, but to live life at its fullest and best. We have already considered the place of faith, and we will reserve prayer for a separate study; here we will take for discussion four words, Love, Truth, Joy, Work, as representing four main highways of life.

Two mistakes we must seek to avoid. First, it is an error to think that there is some one road that we must all take to find life. Life is too rich for that, truth is too varied; and the God whom we seek, the God who is life, is present everywhere. There are more gates than one to the city of God. Second, it is a mistake to suppose that the way to life is an easy one. In the *Survey Graphic* of January, 1929, Donald Richberg wrote about the great scientists, Millikan and Michelson, whom he knew as a student: "Mostly I marveled at the everlasting patience and courage of these men, who won Nobel prizes, not by flashes of genius, but by relentless, unceasing work, illuminated by godlike imagination and sustained by childlike faith." It is not different in the realm of personal life. It has its laws—there is no magic about gaining results here. It makes its demands. The imagination that sees, the faith that trusts and dares, the relentless, unceasing work are even more necessary here than with the scientists. "The utmost for the highest" is its word; and though there is no one way of entrance, the same demand is laid upon us whatever gate we choose.

I. THE WAY OF LOVE

We use love here in its largest sense to include all human fellowship that is marked by good will: the ties of friendship, the intimate relations of the home, affection between opposite sexes, the endless forms of fellowship in which we join with others in work and play and service and worship, and that good will, most like the spirit of Christ, in which we give ourselves and do not think about returns. There is no life for man unless he takes this way. Along this way lie burdens, responsibilities, anxiety, disappointment, sorrow; but apart from this way man cannot find joy, satisfaction, strength, peace, or God. Lose yourself, or you will never find yourself.

Every human life has two sides; it is lived, indeed, in two worlds. There is the world within, the world of my consciousness, of my self-consciousness. There is a "salt, unplumbed, estranging sea" that forever divides that world from even my closest friend. If in that inner world I am not rich and strong, then bonds and broad acres and rich mines and high office would still leave me poor and weak. But here is the paradox: the life within remains poor and mean unless I enter into the full, rich life of the world without, and that means first of all the world of my fellow men. No one ever had such inner resources as Jesus, yet the Gospels show how he too sought and needed the life of fellowship. There were homes where he loved to go as guest, there were friends who ministered to him, there was the inner circle of comrades, the Twelve, who accompanied him everywhere, and within that circle three to whom he felt closest— Peter and James and John. The example of Jesus enforces the lesson of all experience: get outside of yourself, share your life with others, find your life in others.

Love, as we are here using the term, is expressed in many and widely differing forms, but has two common elements. (1) It means good will. When a man begins calculating how much he is going to get out of marriage, or figures how much friends will mean to him in developing his personality or advancing his business, then love is absent and its high rewards as well. Love, in this high sense, is self-forgetting. Selfishness is death, Jesus taught. It is the temptation of us all. Someone has defined the bore as the man who insists upon talking about himself when you want to talk about yourself. Love lifts us out of this, gives life another and higher center of interest, and pushes out beyond the narrow horizons. (2) It means fellowship—sharing, communion, having in common. That means more than a bargain by which we agree, for value received, to help the other man. It is, rather, the generous giving which follows from good will, and which finds its reward in the very act of bestowal. But beyond that, it means in its highest form some faith or loyalty, some task or high devotion which is shared. If a fellowship is to be rich and creative, it must rest upon this common devotion to something higher. No marriage has the promise of happiness or stability, no home the basis for a rich common life, unless there is some high faith and moral idealism which its members share. You may find it with scientists searching after truth, with a group of artists stimulating each other in a common love for beauty and creative effort. Schweitzer, from his hospital in mid-Africa, issues a call for a fellowship of those who sympathize in the service of those who suffer. An enduring and enriching friendship depends absolutely upon finding in common something higher and finer than individual advantage. That is what gives the Church such high possibilities, though so often in practice not realized; for the Church is a fellowship cemented by common faith in God, by common worship, and by union in service. The world of industry will never be redeemed until it ceases to be the strife for selfish advantage, and becomes a common effort to secure to all the needed goods of life.

Thus it is plain how love, or fellowship, becomes a way of life. It redeems us from littleness, it widens life and thus enriches it, it releases the finest elements of human nature, it makes available life's highest goods. The truth of the sage and scientist, the beauty that we all desire, the love without which "the light of the whole world dies," yes, and God himself, all these men can have in very truth only in human fellowship. In the words of the old Persian poet, Firdausi,

"No one could tell me what my soul might be.
I searched for God, and God eluded me.
I sought my brother out and found all three—
My soul, my God, and all humanity."

How can a man know the God who is love if he has
not found the way of love among men? Whittier
sings rightly of "the silence of Eternity interpreted
by love." Nor is it possible here to bring out how
through such fellowship the spirit of man grows finer
in sympathy, purer through affection, how imagination and insight are quickened, and character gains
poise and strength, while on the other hand we take
from our friends comfort in sorrow, courage for
action, with release and healing for pent-up emotions
and hampering inhibitions as we unburden ourselves
to their affection and understanding.

II. The Way of Truth

In the assembly hall of one of our great universities
there used to be on the wall the word from the fourth
Gospel: "Ye shall know the truth, and the truth shall
make you free." Truth is not mere knowledge, not
piled up facts; it deals, rather, with the meaning of
facts. How do these facts hang together? What do
they signify? Where do they point? Here again man
differs from other animals. He challenges the world
of appearance and asks what it means and whither
it is moving. He expresses that in ideas and ideals,
in ends and values. So he finds the meaning and goal
of his own life. This truth becomes a way to life.
It sets us free from fear. It widens our horizons.
The ages are ours, not just this moment of time; ours
are the life of distant lands and the glory of the

heavens. It brings us into a world whose wealth moth and dust do not corrupt, nor thieves break through and steal. And because it reveals our life's meaning and ends, it gives purpose and strength and peace. Someone, contemptuous of his poverty, once referred to Samuel Johnson as "the critic who lives in an alley." To which Johnson responded with the remark about people whose souls lived in an alley. Truth takes the soul out of the alley onto the highway.

Here is where books serve as a way to life. The printed page in itself has no value. Indeed, the flood of speech from press and radio today is one of our perils. What chance is there for the best when the worthless and evil are thus poured out upon us. But if we will resolutely choose and wisely use, what a highway to life books offer us! The reader may say with Emerson:

"I am the owner of the sphere,
 Of the seven stars and the solar year,
 Of Caesar's hand, and Plato's brain,
 Of Lord Christ's heart, and Shakespeare's strain."

Here the immortals of the ages offer themselves to us. They bring their hopes and fears, the insights won through years of searching and noble living. They are the souls who have won through to beauty and truth and God, and they bear it all to us.

The Bible, of course, stands first here. Nowhere else do we find men who have thought so clearly and lived so deeply. As we read them, it is not simply noble ideals of life and high insights into truth that come to us, but a kindling imagination, a stirred heart, a deep desire, a faith created or confirmed—in a word, they bring us face to face with the Eternal who stands everywhere behind time.

But we must not miss the service which other books render. There is biography like Axling's *Kagawa*, or Schweitzer's *Out of My Life and Thought*, or Gandhi's self-revealing autobiography. There are those intimate transcripts of the soul like Augustine's *Confessions*, Amiel's *Private Journal*, or *John Woolman's Journal*. There are the words of the poets, who have known how to wed truth and beauty in a certain inevitability of expression which makes their work the highest creation of man. One might begin with such a collection as *The World's Great Religious Poetry*, selected by Caroline Hill, or the unmatched *Home Book of Verse* edited by Burton Stevenson. History, drama, fiction, all have a claim on us. It is well to gather through the years, one by one, a shelf of books, the friends of the printed page whom you have found of special help.

The way of truth is not without cost to us. It is not the book on the shelf, or the word idly read that counts; it is the truth in heart and mind. These men of the printed page must become our friends; we must live with them. There must be time for quiet and meditation. We must turn back to the same word again and again and carry it with us during the day, if it is to have liberating power in our lives. Honesty, courage, and action are the other great requisites. There must be honesty, the open mind, the courage to face the truth and follow it, despite consequences. We must be like Tennyson's friend, who

> "Would not make his judgment blind,
> Who faced the specters of the mind."

There is no way to truth except through patient search, the single mind, the loyal will. Not lack of knowledge is our weakness, but failure to let the high truth be our constant guest and the ruler of our desire and will. "What we half believe and what we half do, he did utterly," says a recent writer concerning Jesus.

III. THE WAY OF JOY

To some it may seem curious to put among these few paths to life that we have selected for emphasis the way of joy; yet the New Testament has no less than one hundred thirty-five passages that use the word "joy" in some one of its forms, and the Old Testament has even more. The Christ of the fourth Gospel says: "These things have I spoken unto you, that my joy may be in you, and that your joy may be made full." Paul makes the definite demand: "Rejoice in the Lord always; and again I say, rejoice." One of the four tests which the Roman Catholic Church applies before admitting any candidate offered for Sainthood is the note of "expansive joy." And here is an article by an experienced practitioner of medicine and psychotherapy with the title, "The Unhappy Are Always Wrong." The opposite of joy is not sorrow or pain, for a deep and true joy may co-exist with these. It is, rather, what the old teachers called acedia, "a compound of gloom, sloth, and irritation"; and this acedia the Church listed as one of the seven deadly sins. This lack of joy, this apathy, indifference, surliness, is no mere misfortune; it is a wrong way from which we are to turn. On the one side joy is the crown of life, the mark and the fruit of a life that is complete and healthy, physically, morally, mentally, religiously. But it is more than that; it is one of the ways of life toward which we ought to set ourselves, a life that we are to practice, not simply a gift that we are to receive.

Evidently we must distinguish here between joy and pleasure, and particularly between the search for pleasure and the task of joy. Joy is an achievement of the spirit; pleasure is the accompaniment of the physical. Joy has an enduring quality; pleasure passes with its immediate occasion. Joy is essentially unselfish and social in its nature; its cost is not the toil and pain of others, and it grows in the sharing. Pleasure is to be gratefully received when it comes in the normal course; but there is a constant temptation to make it an end of life and to pursue it selfishly. The search for pleasure, as all men know, is self-defeating. It will make more clear what joy is and how it leads to richer life if we note how it comes and what its foes are.

Joy is a summons to forget ourselves, to take thankfully, humbly, appreciatively all that is good and beautiful in the world that God has given us, and to rejoice in it all. Its three great foes are fear, stupidity, and selfishness. A recent story tells of a woman whom fear had shut out from the joys of life. She was afraid of the future, afraid of people, afraid of losing her health and job, afraid of poverty, afraid of herself. And then the doctor told her she had but six months to live. Before this prospect all her little fears vanished and she began really to live, to find joy in all that life had for her—and in the end she found her health as well. The coward dies a hundred deaths before death comes; worry makes slaves of millions and cheats them of the joy that they should have. Faith is part of the way of joy, a trust that looks at life unafraid, as does the child, and rejoices in each gift as it comes.

A second foe is our too great concern with ourselves. Its marks are pride, jealousy, envy, sensitiveness, and that constant comparison with others which leads to the inferiority complex. In a fine novel, *The Coming of the Lord,* Sarah Gertrude Millin depicts a young physician, ambitious, jealous, always comparing himself with real or imagined rivals, always suffering in defeat, until at last he learns to accept himself and stop comparison with others: "Whether anyone else is better or worse," he said, "I am I. Whether I win the race or lose it, my achievement is what it is." To accept ourselves as we are, to see what is ours and find joy in it, better still, to find something higher and finer than our own life and give our life to it and rejoice in it, is the way, not only of escape from unhappiness, but of joy.

Stupidity, insensitiveness, dullness of mind and heart in the presence of beauty and goodness—that is a third hindrance to joy. This is no mere misfortune; it is a sin. Stevenson's lines are worth recalling:

> "If I have faltered more or less
> In my great task of happiness;
> If I have moved among my race
> And shown no glorious morning face;
> If beams from happy human eyes
> Have moved me not; if morning skies,
> Books and my food, and summer rain
> Knocked on my sullen heart in vain:—
> Lord, thy most pointed pleasure take
> And stab my spirit broad awake!"

Every spring is a resurrection from the dead that speaks of the power of the God of life. Every morning is a new creation in which once more we hear him say, "Let there be light." The common gifts of every day renew this summons to gratitude and joy—the tender green of leaves just now unfolding outside my window, the stars into whose depths I looked last night, the rich memory of friends that came to me from the past as I turned over old letters a few days since, the quiet and peace and love of my home. A year or two ago an *Atlantic Monthly* correspondent wrote of a "summer in London amid a political and economic world unutterably disheartening. At its nadir I became suddenly conscious of a world of beauty about me." It began with an ancient Chinese vase, with glory of color and grace of curve, and led to a notebook page headed, "Things of Beauty," with a long list that included items as varied as the curve of a ploughshare, Dean Lutkin's "Choral Blessing," the hymn "Where cross the crowded ways of life," Captain Scott's last letter to Barrie, and the laughter of little children at play. Beauty, after love, is one of the greatest of the summons to joy.

To this let us add the thought of joy in God. Here is the deepest cause for joy and one that always waits for us. It lies in Wordsworth's phrase about "a presence that disturbs me with the joy of elevated thought." It is a summons to high imagination. It lifts us out of the narrow round and the selfish interest. It bids us call to mind what God means: the order that spans the measureless heavens and reaches to the swift whirling electrons of the invisible atom, the beauty that is of the very texture of being, the majesty of high holiness, the sure justice that bids us face all threats of evil unafraid, the infinite good will that reaches each least human life. To dwell on all this in wonder and worship and joy is to find one of the great highways of life.

IV. The Way of Work

Work is a way of life. Not drudgery—drudgery is work that has no meaning, that is carried on in the spirit of the slave; but work rightly conceived is a way of life for which there is no substitute. Such work is, first of all, necessary for health of body and mind. Like a machine running without a "load" and racking itself to pieces, so is a human life that has not found work to do or that will not do its work. The energy of body and spirit remain, but the nervous force turns in upon itself in restless thought, in unsatisfied desires, and brings inner disintegration and social maladjustment. War experience with shell-shock cases and the insights of applied psychology have shown work to be one of the great curative means. The educator, the psychotherapist, the social worker dealing with the physically handicapped or facing the terrible results in moral deterioration which come from enforced idleness, all realize that work is a supreme necessity for a wholesome, happy, socially adjusted, and rightly developing life.

But beyond all that, work is a way of fellowship with God. Ours is not a God who sits aloft, serene, unmoved, unmoving. He is Creative Good Will, the Energy that toils ceaselessly to carry out high ends. How can men enter into his life except as they share that life in work motivated by good will? So man becomes cocreative with God. "My Father worketh until now; and I work." An ancient papyrus, found in Egypt and purporting to give sayings of Jesus, has these words: "When two are together, they are not without God, and where one is alone, behold! I am with him. Lift the stone and thou shalt find me; cleave the wood and there am I." He who will may find fellowship with God in the humblest task. There is a poem of Rabindranath Tagore, in his volume, *Gitanjali,* where he summons the worshiper, if he would find God, to leave the dark temple and seek him where men are at work.

He is there where the tiller is tilling the hard ground and where the pathmaker is breaking stones. He is with them in sun and in shower, and his garment is covered with dust.

Come out of thy meditations and leave aside thy flowers and incense! What harm is there if thy clothes become tattered and stained? Meet him and stand by him in toil and in sweat of thy brow.

We have considered the ways of life. They are all of them equally ways to the knowledge of God, ways by which men may enter into fellowship with God. For God himself is love and truth and beauty and joy and creative good will.

———

QUESTIONS FOR DISCUSSION

Select a number of people from among those known to you personally who seem to have achieved a rich and satisfying life: what are the ways which they have followed? If possible, inquire of them.

What ways have you found personally of greatest help in

gaining insight, overcoming temptation, securing the sense of the reality of God and fellowship with him, finding inner strength and peace and joy, overcoming inner discord and gaining inner unity?

From those whom you know personally or through your reading, select at least one example to illustrate each of the ways of life discussed in this chapter.

What other ways of help would you add to those here discussed?

FOR FURTHER READING

Some of the books listed with the last two chapters and the next following are of value for this chapter also.

R. C. Cabot: *What Men Live By*
Rufus M. Jones: *The Inner Life; Spiritual Energies*
Kirby Page: *Living Creatively; Living Triumphantly*
H. N. Wieman: *Methods of Private Religious Living*
L. D. Weatherhead: *Jesus and Ourselves; Discipleship*
The Journal of John Woolman
Brother Lawrence: *The Practice of the Presence of God*
Caroline M. Hill: *The World's Great Religious Poetry*
Michael I. Pupin: *The New Reformation* (closing chapter)

XV

PRAYER

"WHY do men pray?" William James was once asked. "Because they cannot help it," was his answer. The impulse to prayer has two sides, a "push" and a "pull." On the human side there is a "push," the drive of our needs and desires. At its lowest that may be a selfish wish, at its highest it is that dissatisfaction with what is, that aspiration toward life at its richest and fullest, which is the noblest side of man. But there is also a "pull" in prayer, a movement from above. The tides of the Spirit beat upon these shores of humanity. Prayer is not simply a search but a response. If there had been no kindling light, there would be no searching eye. If there were no Spirit of the Eternal, quickening the human soul, there would be none of that feeling of need, that sense of something Higher, out of which prayer comes. Not many men pray intelligently and effectively, but there are few if any who have not in some manner or at some time lifted their hearts in prayer.

I. WHAT IS PRAYER?

Religion is life in fellowship with the Eternal; prayer is fellowship with God coming to conscious expression. To pray is to turn our thought to God. We sometimes define prayer rather loosely. Prayer is supreme desire, we are told. "To labor is to pray," runs an ancient word. Both are true but only part

of the truth. Labor may be prayer, but only as it is
linked in thought and purpose to God. True prayer
is supreme desire, but supreme desire may be wholly
selfish and earthly, with no relation to God and no
meaning as prayer.

Fellowship with God has many forms; it should be
as broad as life. In prayer we enter consciously into
the presence of God. Even so, prayer means many
different things. Brother Lawrence was a simple
lay brother who served in a monastery in France long
years ago. In a little pamphlet, *The Practice of the
Presence of God,* he tells his experience with prayer.
He found the regular hours and forms of prayer difficult and not helpful, so he learned how to make his
humble tasks in the kitchen the occasion for conscious
fellowship with God. Prayer may take that form. To
pause a moment on a summer morning, to rejoice in
its light and life, in "the solemn hush of nature newly
born," and then to lift the soul in thanksgiving or worship—that is prayer. To wait a moment for help as
we turn to some difficult task or trying experience,
in the midst of busy toil to offer up our work to God
—that is prayer. To hush the soul in reverent awe as
we look up into the stars, to lift it in joy as we see the
glory of sunset color, to breathe a word of gratitude
as we turn from our daily work to the love and peace
of our homes—that is prayer.

1. Prayer has two sides, a double movement
which corresponds to the "push" and "pull" of
prayer. It means first bringing our life to God. To
pray is to take our whole life, its joys and needs, its
desires and failures, into the presence of the Infinite.
Thanksgiving, confession, penitence, and petition all

belong here. Yet even on this side, the center of prayer is not our life but God. The important matter is not this bringing of our life and its concerns to God; it is what happens to us when we bring them. We bring the good things of life in gratitude, and life becomes richer and more joyous when we see them as his gift. We bring our sins and failures, seeing our true self in the light of God, yet trusting in his infinite mercy; we leave with divided souls united, with hearts healed by forgiveness, with courage for a new start. We bring our bitterness and resentment, our jealousies and hurts—all those feelings and attitudes which give rise to maladjustment and unhappiness; we go, our spirits changed by his Spirit into the peace and good will of Christ.

2. Prayer is bringing God to our life. The greatest misunderstandings and failures in prayer have their source in our making ourselves and our desires the center of prayer. As Elizabeth Herman puts it in her *Creative Prayer:* "Is the central element in our communion with God an act of self-surrender, or is it a demand of self-love? Is the symbol of our prayer the open hand or the open heart? Are we using God as a means of self-realization, or are we offering ourselves as a means of glorifying him?" It is a curious paradox: prayer is the greatest means of self-realization, but we fail in this if prayer keeps self as the center. It is significant that the first half of the Lord's Prayer is all centered in God: "Our Father, who art in heaven, hallowed be thy name, thy kingdom come, thy will be done." Only after this do man and his needs come in.

The need of this side of prayer is obvious. The

world of things crowds upon us every moment of the day. "The primary object of worship," wrote the late Charles A. Bennett of Yale, "seems to me to be the recovery in the midst of secular routine of this sense of the nearness of the mysterious power and the getting into right relation with it. God is always there: in the press of daily living he is lost to view: worship is the deliberate lifting up of the heart to him again. Religion is a perpetual rediscovery of God."

Clearly, prayer so conceived is no easy matter of words idly spoken. As Paul Sabatier writes in his *Saint Francis of Assisi:* "To pray is to talk with God, to lift ourselves up to him, to converse with him, that he may come down to us. It is an act of meditation, of reflection, which presupposes the effort of all that is most personal in us. With Saint Francis, as with Jesus, prayer has this character of effort which makes of it the greatest moral act. For him, as for his Master, the end of prayer is communion with the heavenly Father, the accord of the divine with the human; or rather, it is man who puts forth his strength to do the work of God, not saying to him a mere passive, resigned, powerless, 'Thy will be done,' but courageously raising his head: 'Behold me, Lord, I delight to do thy will.'"

II. The Laws of Prayer

There are certain principles, or laws, underlying prayer which must be considered if prayer is to be effective. There is no magic in prayer; there is order in the world of spirit as truly as in the world of nature. If a battery is dead, you cannot expect power; if a connection is broken you will not get light. Even so you will not become a saint over night just because you prayed, "Lord, make me good." Prayer does not cut across the order of God, it fits into it. Our understanding of this order and our adjustment to its forces make possible that life-giving relation with God which is the concern of prayer. Here are five laws that we may consider.

1. The law of attention has two sides. (1) We must attend if we would know. The physical world exercises its power on us whether we will or no; the light that beats down, the sounds that assail our ears, the air that we breathe—these come to us whether we consider them or not. It is not so with the world of spiritual forces and values. These can reach us only as we attend to them. Beauty and love and truth are ours only as we turn thought and desire toward them. Only so can God enter into human life. "Behold, I stand at the door and knock." Our interest, our thought, our quickened imagination are doors for God's entrance. (2) We become like that to which we attend; and as we turn our thought persistently to the world of the Spirit we are transformed by it. No mere act of the will is enough. "When the will and imagination are at war," writes Baudouin, in his *Suggestion and Autosuggestion,* "the imagination invariably gains the day." The frontal attack on evil is not enough; the flank movement is needed. Direct your thought systematically to what is good, and you will conquer. Prayer is attention. "We all, with unveiled face, beholding as in a mirror the glory of the Lord, are

transformed into the same image" (2 Corinthians 3. 18).

2. The law of desire. Prayer is supreme desire consciously and constantly voiced. "Prayer represents the daily expression to oneself of the right thing to do," said Cecil Rhodes. And the law of desire is that we gradually become what we most deeply long for. What a man most wants is really his prayer, no matter what his lips may frame. In Emerson's words,

> "And though thy knees were never bent,
> To heaven thy hourly prayers are sent;
> And, whether formed for good or ill,
> Are registered and answered still."

What we need, if the highest is to be realized, is to look each day at the goals for which we strive, to examine them in the light of the Eternal, and to affirm and reaffirm our supreme desire.

3. The law of trust and devotion is this, that courage and strength and peace come only to him who has found that to which he can give himself in confidence and surrender. "In returning and rest shall ye be saved," wrote the prophet, "in quietness and in confidence shall be your strength." As George Mac-Donald put it in *Robert Falconer:* "This is a healthy, a practical, a working faith. First, that a man's business is to do the will of God. Second, that God takes upon himself the care of that man. Third, and therefore, that a man ought never to be afraid of anything." The prayer which affirms this trust and devotion is the highest preparation for fruitful action.

4. The law of persistence. There is truth in the homely saying: "It's dogged as does it." There is

an easily misunderstood parable of Jesus which tells of the unjust judge who granted the poor widow's plea not because she was right or he was good, but because she would not give up. God is not an unconcerned or unjust Ruler who can be driven to action by our persistence; it is for our own sake that the persistence is needed. In prayer it is no casual, idle request that brings results; it is an unswerving desire kept constantly to the fore. Patiently and persistently we must hold certain things before us. Again and again we must voice our trust in God and affirm the goals that we seek. There are goals of life that some of us can never reach, despite all seeking: a fortune of a million, the genius of a Shakespeare or an Einstein. But the greatest goods are open to us all—peace of soul, strength for the day's task, power to rule ourselves, love for men, faith in God. Only, we must pay the cost, and persistence is a part of that price.

III. The Practice of Prayer

In one sense prayer is as simple as breathing or eating. What is more natural than for the child to speak to its Father? Yet prayer is an art too, perhaps the greatest art that can engage man. It is one that demands all that we can offer of thought and will, of imagination and devotion; and a lifetime is not too long to learn how to pray. Perhaps the highest art of prayer is when man learns to "pray without ceasing," so to live with God that one may turn to him at any moment of the day, to "practice the presence of God." But for most men, if not all, there is need of some regular period specially given to devotion, and of guidance in the use of that time. Here are some suggestions gathered from those who have practiced this art and reflected upon it. They can be put in five words.

1. Relaxation. In prayer we enter into the presence of God; let us then leave behind all anxieties and cares. Relax physically and mentally. To have a quiet place and a definite, unhurried period of time will greatly help. One might join that group of French mystics whose simple rule was, "A quarter hour for God." The aim is quietness of mind, not emptiness; not inertness or passivity, but a turning away from other concerns that we may be open to the tides of the spirit.

2. Meditation. It is easy to hurry too quickly to the act of prayer. When we bring little, we take little; "to him that hath shall be given." Our prayers are often meaningless because our minds are empty. We need quickening of mind, kindling of spirit, stirring of imagination, widening of horizon. Meditation is not daydreaming. If you have fifteen minutes for devotion, spend at least ten in reading and reflection. You cannot meditate on nothing. Find the best that the great spirits can offer you. Use the Bible, hymns, prayers, poetry, biography—but do not merely read; let their thoughts stir you and start your spirit on its way. You will not go far till you will find yourself praying.

3. Realization. A single word can hardly express this. Some speak of it as recollection. It is akin to the practice of the presence of God. Dwell with the thought of the God who is "closer . . . than breathing, and nearer than hands and feet." Call before

your mind his goodness in which you can utterly
trust, his power which holds all things. Prayer is
more than your search for him; his search for you
comes first. There would be no praying if he had not
first sought you and found you. The need which
drives you to prayer is the mark of his presence. A
writer, telling his experience in learning to pray, says
that, until a time of stress came to him, though he
had heard prayers and said prayers without number,
he found he did not know how to pray. "I seemed to
be talking into thin air. I was not aware of a listen-
ing God at all. The whole experience was nebulous
and unreal. The first stage of progress was that of
coming to feel that a higher Power was present,
knew that I spoke, heard my words with sympa-
thetic attention. It was a great deal, a very great
deal, to attain as much as this." Inseparable from
such realization will be adoration and worship, which
is the very heart of prayer. "Religion is adoration,"
Baron Von Hügel used to say. "Prayer is the lifting
up of the mind to God." To find the highest and
bow before it is the supreme experience of religion,
and worship is its purest expression.

4. Examination. We need to look at ourselves in
prayer. "I have prayed in my day, like others,"
writes Robert Louis Stevenson in his *Journal*, "for
wicked, foolish, or senseless alterations in the scheme
of things. But these groping complaints are not
prayer. It is in prayer that a man resumes his attitude toward God and the world; the thought of his
heart comes out of him clean and simple; he takes,
in Shakespeare's language, a new acquaintance of
himself and makes of that a new point of departure

in belief and conduct." We need to face honestly the facts of our life, to scrutinize our habits and our attitudes, to see what is there of impurity of thought, of sensitiveness and jealousy, of ill will or bitterness in relation to others; not that we may dwell on this morbidly, but that we may take forgiveness from God, find his purpose for us, and go forward to a new life.

5. Affirmation. Every prayer is an act of will in which we affirm once more that which we desire and devote ourselves anew to God. It is not enough that we once made the great decision, that once we determined to lead the Christian life and follow what was true and good. In the world of busy cares and selfish strife our ideals grow vague in outline and weak in power. We need each day to see anew the meaning of life, and what it is that we really want to be and do. And we need to make that specific; quiet of mind, deep trust instead of anxious care, patience and kindliness where we have been irritable, a deeper sense of God, more concern for our fellow men—we must set before ourselves definite ends like these for each day. Here too repetition may come in. A man won his victory over an unruly temper by training himself to repeat habitually: "The fruit of the Spirit is love, joy, peace, longsuffering, kindness, goodness, faithfulness, meekness, self-control."

These five steps of prayer are like

> "The world's great altar stairs,
> That slope through darkness up to God."

They are not meant to be mechanically followed; no one can prescribe an order of prayer like that They do represent tried ways by which to approach God. But it will take time and thought and patient practice to make them yield their full fruit, and each must learn to use them in his own way.

IV. What Shall We Ask For?

I have left for the last the matter which so often is put first. Prayer is fellowship with God, not just asking things from God; and yet petition has a place in prayer. What, then, shall I ask for: my child's recovery, rain in time of drought, success in business? And what may I expect? The Christian position can be set forth in a few words. 1. Bring everything to God—health, business, loved ones, everything. There is nothing which concerns his children in which a father is not interested. 2. Leave everything with God. That is what faith in God means, that we can trust him absolutely in all things. There is nothing which we should so much desire as his will, no good that we should so much crave as God himself. Prayer is not insistence upon our own will but devotion to his; it is not confidence in our petition but in his goodness and wisdom. 3. Expect great things from God—not everything that we wish, certainly not everything that we ask for, but what we need most and what God can do for us under the given conditions. God is the God of order, an order which has its being in his own nature of truth and wisdom; he cannot turn this world from cosmos to chaos to suit our individual wish, and for our sake and the world's sake he will not. That is not what Jesus meant by his "Ask, and it shall be given unto you." What he meant was that God had vastly more to give us than we think or dare to ask. Pray, and expect great things from God.

QUESTIONS FOR DISCUSSION

Wrong ideas as to prayer, and wrong practices.
The different forms which prayer may take.
Helpful methods in the life of prayer.
Books that help and how to use them.
Chief difficulties in the practice of prayer.
Difficulties in the idea of prayer.
Beliefs that are implied in prayer.
Why men pray.
What can prayer do for men?

FOR FURTHER READING

Harry Emerson Fosdick: *The Meaning of Prayer*
W. P. Paterson, Editor: *The Power of Prayer*
William Adams Brown: *The Life of Prayer in an Age of Science*
Samuel McComb: *Prayer, What It Is and What It Does*
Glenn Clark: *The Soul's Sincere Desire*
Margaret P. Montague: *Twenty Minutes of Reality*
B. H. Streeter, Editor: *Concerning Prayer*
W. Rauschenbusch: *Prayers of the Social Awakening*
Mary W. Tilleston: *Prayers, Ancient and Modern*
W. E. Orchard: *The Temple*
Samuel McComb: *A Book of Modern Prayers*
Friedrich Heiler: *Prayer*

XVI

THE MEANING AND PLACE OF THE BIBLE

I. YESTERDAY AND TODAY

A GENERATION or two ago the question about the Bible would have been answered very simply: "The Bible is the Word of God. God gave it to men as the revelation of himself. He inspired it, so it is infallible. It is not only the word of God to man but the words of God, and our duty is simply to believe every word and obey every command."

The answer is not so simple today, and the reason is not because men have become skeptical and irreligious; it is, rather, because men have been studying the Bible itself and learning from the Bible itself what it is. If any one thing characterizes the modern mind, it is the empirical attitude: look for the facts and let the theory follow. So men faced certain facts that made impossible the old theory of a book verbally inspired and infallible. The Old Testament is not all on a level. It has lofty conceptions of God, but there is here also the picture of a God who demanded that when a certain city was captured in war, its walls and buildings should be leveled, its trees cut down, its cattle destroyed, and every man, woman, and child should be put to death. Not all the atrocity stories, the propaganda which people swallowed during the World War, contained anything more terrible than that. There are noble words here which call for mercy and good will reaching to

all men, but here also are the words which Jesus had
to repudiate though they were given in "the law":
"An eye for an eye and a tooth for a tooth." You
cannot accept the supremacy of Christ and hold to
the infallibility of the Bible.

The interesting fact is that in spite of all this the
Bible did not lose its place. Men still found God in
the Bible, and the guidance and strength for life.
Some parts they simply passed by, others they read
in the light of the highest that it offered. In times
of sorrow, they did not read Ecclesiastes, with its
terrible words: "Man hath no preeminence above the
beasts: as the one dieth, so dieth the other." They
turned to John fourteen: "In my Father's house
there are many dwelling places." They knew the
vindictive psalms were in the Bible, those psalms
which John Wesley declared were "highly improper
for the mouths of a Christian congregation," in which
the writer calls for vengeance upon his enemy, asks
that his very prayer be turned into sin, demands vengeance even upon the children: "Happy shall he be,
that taketh and dasheth thy little ones against the
rock." They read instead of the pity of Jesus in the
midst of the agony of death: "Father, forgive them,"
and of his summons that we should be merciful like
our Father in heaven. The Bible is a greater book
than man's theories about it. Here are imperishable
treasures suited to man's need, here men still hear
the living God calling to them. So men keep on
reading the Bible today. Not in all the centuries
have more copies been printed than today. There is
hardly an obscure tribe in whose language it does not
appear, and year by year in the centers of culture it

sells more copies than any "best seller" in its brief day. Let us, then, look at it afresh, leave our theories behind, and try to see it as it is.

II. THE BOOK OF GOD AND THE BOOK OF MAN

The Bible is a human book; it is not something dropped from the skies, it has come out of the life of men. Here are man's hopes and fears, his prayers and tears, his struggles and victories and defeats, his search for God and his joy in finding God and in fellowship with him. It is, indeed, the most human of books. "Prick it anywhere and it will bleed." The Old Testament is the literature of a people: laws, history, prayers, poems, hymns, sermons, all are here. Some of these books tell the story of the people, others grew directly out of the experience of individual men, and in them they pour forth the wealth of what they have been given to see and learn. Indeed, for us "the Old Testament has been changed from a file of books into a line of men." We are not, then, surprised to find limitations here and differences, the fallible and partial. That belongs, necessarily, to whatever is human.

But men find the Bible a divine book today, just as their fathers did. It is still the Word of God to man. What do we mean by that? With what right do we use these old terms? Once more let us look frankly at the facts. Let any man come to these writings with an open mind, an eager desire to know the living God and the way of life: what will he find? Much that will not mean anything to him, some that will even repel him, as we have seen; but as he reads psalms and prophets, the Gospels and other parts of the New Testament, something more than human will come to him.

(1) He will gain a vision of God, the sense of one who is high and holy and yet who is intimately present in his world, who is righteousness and truth and yet who compasses in his love the least of his creatures and goes out in mercy to the most evil of men. God is never made real by argument. Religion is caught rather than taught. He will not find here a book of theory, but one of life: by the faith of these men, by their deep experience of God, by the passion of their lives, his own heart will be stirred. It will be more than an idea of God: the reality of God will confront him. The God who spoke to them will speak to him, and he too will say, "I saw the Lord high and lifted up."

(2) He will gain a new vision of life, of what life means, what it may become, what it must be. Human life will seem to him, in the light of this God, no longer something poor and mean and hopeless, but something high and sacred, for it has come from God and it belongs to him. He will see the high purpose of each man's life and of humanity. Above all, he will discover a new kind of life, the only kind, life according to the spirit of this God. Olive Schreiner tells how as a little girl in her South-African home she first read the Gospels. Her mind opened up, she caught the picture of life as it appears in the Sermon on the Mount, and in her new enthusiasm she rushed in to her mother and cried: "Oh, Mummy, look what I've found: isn't it lovely? Now we can all live like this." The wood where Count Tolstoy was buried, so his son tells us, was one where his

brother Nicholas used to play as a child and where he once "buried a little stick on which he had written a secret talisman that would make all people happy. It was the one word—Love." All this he will find here.

(3) He will find himself here. "In the volume of the book it is written of me." "What other book like this," writes Sabatier, "can awaken dumb or sleeping consciences, reveal the secret needs of the soul, sharpen the thorn of sin and press its cruel point upon us, tear away our delusions, humiliate our pride, and disturb our false serenity? What sudden lightnings it shoots into the abysses of our hearts! What searchings of conscience are like those which we make by this light!" But every man is two men, the man that is and the man that is to be; and this second man is revealed here also—"all we have willed, or hoped, or dreamed of good," and more— the man that God wants us to be.

(4) And he will find here a book of power. That, after all, is our deepest need in religion. "All the high maxims have been uttered," remarked Pascal once; "now we have only to obey them"—and there's the rub. But we may confidently say: He who will search out what is highest in this book, who will live with it so that it has a real chance at his mind and heart and imagination, and who will give himself in obedience when the Highest here speaks to him, he will find here the power of a new life.

Here then is why we call this the book of God: it is the story of how God spoke to men in the past; by it he speaks to men today; through it he still works as a life-giving and life-changing power.

III. Theories Old and New

The fact of the Bible is one thing, its moral and spiritual significance, its historical and literary forms; the theories about the Bible are another matter. Our fathers knew that God was in this history and that God spoke to them through these words; that was fact. But the scholars were not so happy in their theories. The main difficulty was in not understanding how God worked in his world. They thought of God as above his world. God's word when he spoke to men they conceived as something coming from without, as when a man speaks to his fellow. Revelation meant to them so many doctrines or commandments handed down, or so many words dictated to a writer. In a word they made revelation intellectual in content, external and mechanical in method. At both points they missed the historical and vital and spiritual.

What the Bible actually shows us, and what our experience reveals to us, is something quite different. Life comes first, ideas and words follow, whether you think of God's side or man's. *Religion in Life* is the happily chosen name of a great journal, for religion is life. God comes to men first not as a Voice but as a Presence. Israel finds him in her history, and the prophets tell her what this history means, what God is doing, what he is saying through these triumphs and defeats. It is just so in the New Testament. The Christian religion did not begin with words from God which were put into a book; it began with God's presence, his deeds, his power. "God was in Christ," Paul says. "The Word became flesh,"

John writes, "and dwelt among us; and we beheld his glory, full of grace and truth." The first words of this Gospel might well be translated, as Goethe has it in his *Faust*: "In the beginning was the deed." It was so after the death of Christ; a new life stirred this company of disciples, a new power of faith and love made different men of them and drove them forth to high deeds. To some among them it was given, by a Spirit greater than themselves, to understand what all this meant, to see God in it all; and so they wrote these letters and Gospels that make up the New Testament. But the life came first, and the writings came out of the life.

Of course these men were no more infallible in their ideas than they were perfect in life. Peter and Paul differed vigorously and with feeling. Paul thought, quite like the men of his time, that a woman should be subject to her husband, should keep silent in the church, and have her head covered. We do not follow him there. We see he was mistaken in thinking that the Lord would return in a few years in visible form to establish his kingdom on earth. When Paul wrote to his little churches here and there to settle their quarrels and inspire their faith, he surely had not the faintest idea that centuries later theologians would be building up their theories on this phrase or that sentence in his letters. But Paul did know that God had come to men in Jesus Christ and had revealed to them what he was and what they might become; and he set that forth in no uncertain terms. He remains for us, as he was for them, a great preacher of this message, and through his words this same living God comes to us.

Men have declared that the Bible was inspired. Inspiration means the presence and working of the Spirit of God. Strictly speaking, not the writings were inspired but the writers. But greater and more important, and prior to all writing, was God's deed and presence, his movement in Israel's history, in the heart of prophet and psalmist, in Jesus and his followers. These writings grew out of this redemptive movement of God and were a part of it, written by men who saw what it all meant; and the same stream of divine life and light comes to us today through them and through the fellowship of the church.

IV. How Shall We Use the Bible?

What special place and authority, then, do these writings have? We shall do no service to the truth if we declare that only in the Bible is there light, that elsewhere all is darkness, that only in Israel did God come to men, that in all other peoples and all other faiths we have only man's vain search for God. To say this would be to be untrue to the Bible itself and to the revelation of God in Christ. Can we have so narrow a vision of God as to think that he concerned himself only with one little people among the teeming millions, and only for one brief span of years in the long ages? Or can we be so Pharisaic as to suppose that only in our limited succession have there been minds to grasp and hearts to respond to God? Paul had a larger vision when he spoke of a God who had not left himself without a witness; and eight hundred years earlier the prophets wrote of one who was the God of all peoples, who had not only brought Israel from Egypt but the Philistines from

Caphtor and the Syrians from Kir, who anointed
Cyrus as he had David before him. The God of our
Lord Jesus Christ is the God who has sought out
every nation and waited at the door of every heart.
And we rejoice in all the light that can be found in
other faiths, for there is only one truth and all truth
is of God.

And yet we must face certain simple facts. God
waits at the door, he does not break in. Here was a
people whose passion was God, as the passion of
other peoples lay in war or wisdom or letters or art
or trade. Here was a line of men, the prophets,
whose devotion to righteousness and whose vision of
God have made them the teachers of the nations
through the ages. Within a single generation in this
little land we find no less than four of these great
names: Isaiah, Amos, Hosea, and Micah. But above
all, it is through these writings that we know Jesus
Christ. He is their center and he makes them unique.
A few years ago H. G. Wells suggested that humanity urgently needed a new Bible. He pointed out
that once our Western world was united because it
had a common Bible and owned its authority; but
now east and west formed one world and the God of
the Bible commanded neither west nor east. That
is true, but where on humanity's horizon is there a
faith, a vision of God, or an ideal of life for men or
nations that can for a moment challenge what is
found here? There will never be peace or justice in
the world till men own one common God, but it will
not come through a new Bible.

But another question rises; is not the authority of
the Bible gone if we cannot say of every word that

it is the word of God? Why should we follow it, or
how shall we know what to accept?

There are two kinds of authority. One is external,
compulsive. It does not ask for understanding or
conviction, but simply submission. The other is
inner, moral, spiritual; it asks obedience, but the
obedience must root in conviction and come as free
choice. The former belongs to subjects, the latter
to sons. Free men know only one kind of authority—
that of truth and right. For the Christian that
means God, for God is righteousness and truth. The
final authority for our faith is God, and God alone.
The Bible is authority for us only in so far as it
brings God, only so far as through the Spirit of God
it wakens conviction in our hearts. Mohammedanism, Mormonism, and Christian Science are book religions. Christianity is the religion of the living God
as we know him in Jesus Christ; it has a book, but
it is not a book religion. The Bible does have authority. It has wielded that year after year. Men have
hearkened to it for this one reason, because it has
convinced men of its truth and brought God to men.

And this suggests how we shall use the Bible and
what we shall follow. (1) There is a Spirit that
guides men into the truth. Ask for that guidance,
read with an open mind, follow with an obedient
will. You will have questions here and there, but
the highway of faith and life will stretch plain before
you. (2) The Bible has a center toward which the
old tends, from which the new flows—Jesus Christ.
Bring all else to that test, make him supreme. (3)
But of one thing make sure: read it, use it. Live in
its atmosphere. Let its great words become your

familiar friends.   It can stand question, criticism, opposition, everything but neglect.

QUESTIONS FOR DISCUSSION

In what significant sense may we call the Bible the book of God? The book of man?

Aldous Huxley, in his *Brave New World,* writes of an imaginary future world from which the Bible is banished with Shakespeare and all the old classics: What would we lose if the Bible were wholly eliminated from the knowledge and use of men?

What are the chief values of the Bible to individual life? To society?

Why do not people use the Bible more or get more from it?

What are the best methods for the personal use of the Bible?

FOR FURTHER READING

Harry Emerson Fosdick: *The Modern Use of the Bible*

H. F. Rall: *Modern Premillennialism,* Chaps. VII, IX

A. S. Peake: *The Bible, Its Origin, Significance, and Abiding Worth*

C. H. Dodd: *The Authority of the Bible*

See general articles on Bible, Old Testament, New Testament, Literature of the Bible, etc., in Hastings' *D. B.* and other Bible dictionaries, and in the *Abingdon Bible Commentary,* or Peake's *Commentary on the Bible*

XVII

I BELIEVE IN THE CHURCH

I. THE INEVITABLE CHURCH

THE Church is under criticism today. Men charge that it stands for outworn ideas, that it is not adjusted to modern needs, that it lacks moral and spiritual dynamic, that its constant temptation is to save itself instead of serving humanity, that by its unconcern, if not its opposition, it is a hindrance to social progress. More even than criticism, the Church suffers from indifference. Men feel that it is an anachronism, belonging to an earlier age where men were concerned not with life here on earth, but only with saving their souls and getting to heaven. And so they pass it by.

There is, of course, nothing new in this. The Church has always met with criticism and suffered from indifference; and the criticism has been needed. Yet it is the Church that nurtured the saints of the ages, that gave birth to schools and hospitals and every manner of philanthropy and reform, that stirred men with vision and sent them out to serve, that handed on the Old Testament and gave birth to the New. The Church, the Church alone, preserved for humanity the highest treasure that has come from the past, the picture of Jesus and the story of his words and life. And when the Church needed criticism and reform, when faith hardened into dogma, and formalism and selfishness deadened its spirit, it was from within the Church that the men came who challenged its evils and brought it to a new birth.

The reason why the Church is inevitable lies in the very nature of life itself. The Church is religion in its group expression, religion as an organic, a corporate affair. We have seen again and again how important this principle of organicism is. Life everywhere is a matter of wholes; there is no place in this world for the merely individual. Separation is death; association is the way of life. If you want to be a whole, you must belong to a whole. The higher you advance in the scale of life the more significant that principle becomes. The church is the fellowship of men on the highest level of life, that of religion. To expect religion to be rich and strong without such a fellowship is to deny the principle that runs through life everywhere.

If Christianity is the highest form of religion, then we may expect it to give a large place to this aspect of fellowship. The New Testament shows two striking facts. One is that it contains neither any command to organize the Church nor any rules about its constitution and government. The other is that from the beginning Christianity was a fellowship. It was no specific command but the very nature of the new life that brought that with it: the loyalty to a common Lord, the faith which impelled the disciples to common worship and service, the spirit of love which bound them together. Further, they were sure that this common life of theirs was something divine. They had a profound experience of a certain Presence in their midst, of something greater than themselves. They thought of it as the divine Spirit, or Holy Spirit, as the spirit or presence of Christ, or simply as God among them and within them. It was no mere individual affair; it was a life that belonged to them as the "family of God," the "body of Christ." The Church has never been the result of human decision or divine command, but the inevitable expression of the life of Christianity.

II. What Is the Church?

In an earlier chapter we studied the nature of Christianity. There we saw two broadly differing conceptions. We called the one the institutional, the other the spiritual, or vital-historical. Broadly considered, the theories of the nature of the Church divide along the same lines. The most thoroughgoing expression of the institutional conception is in the Roman Church. The Roman-Catholic teaching is somewhat as follows: In religion man needs to know what to believe, how to live, and how to be saved. These three needs Christ met as prophet bringing truth, as king bearing rule and precept, as priest offering salvation. This threefold authority and power he left to the Church, which he established to carry on his work, more particularly to the Twelve with Peter at their head, and to their successors, the bishops, with the bishop of Rome (the pope) in Peter's stead. Thus we have the Church as an institution, "external of its own nature and visible," as Pope Pius declared in his encyclical of 1928, having infallible authority in teaching and rule and charge of the means of salvation through the sacraments. The Church is thus a single visible institution, divine and inerrant.

Against this stands the spiritual, or vital-historical theory. This is no merely humanistic conception; the Church is not just an organization which a group of men decided upon. It is divine, but the divine element is not a legally prescribed and supernaturally established ecclesiastical institution; it is a spirit and a life that entered this world with Christ and has lived on as a creative power in his followers. What Jesus left behind, as Archbishop Temple has pointed out, "was not an organized society with constitution and rules; nor was it a book which he had written for the guidance of his disciples; but it was a group of disciples united to one another by their common allegiance to him. It was a living fellowship." Religion here is divine, not merely human; it is corporate, not merely individual. It has its institutional side: ritual, sacraments, officiary, rules, creeds; but these are the outgrowth of the life, here to serve it, not dominate it, and to be changed when needed.

III. The Function of the Church

We can best understand the nature of the Church, its place in religion, and its claim on men by asking what its function is in religion.

1. It is the prophetic Church, the Church with a message. Men are skeptical today about ideas; they call for deeds, not words; for life and not doctrine. Jesus was nearer the truth when he said, "Man shall not live by bread alone." The choice is not between words and deeds; it is, rather, whether our action shall be as brutes impelled by blind passion, or as men guided by ideas and purposes. The first and greatest gift of the Church is its message. That was all that

those first humble men had who went forth into the Roman Empire nineteen centuries ago. With that message they faced Roman power and Grecian culture. With it they spoke to the needs of human souls and kindled a new hope in humanity. With it they confronted ancient evils and created a new conscience for king and commoner. And when, at last, the walls of empire crumbled and its armies melted away before the onset of the tribes of the north, it was the foundations laid by these men that withstood the shock; it was their message that conquered the conquerors, and their ideals that gave order to the new age.

Our need is just as great today. It is not bread alone for which men are hungering. "What does life mean?" they cry. "What can I hope for? Where can I turn for light?" There is no answer in the pessimism and naturalism of our day. In its hopeless creed,

> "The world rolls round forever like a mill,
> It grinds out death and life and good and ill,
> It has no purpose, heart, or mind, or will."

The Church comes with a historic revelation, with One in whom word became deed, and through whose deed the living God has spoken to men. It bids the common man look up and say, Our Father. It bids him look out and see a world that he can face without fear. It holds up an ideal that at once commands his loyalty and gives his life meaning and hope. Its message is just as necessary for the social order. "In general the forces that go to make up public opinion in this country are narrow and selfish," says President Hutchins, of the University of Chicago. "They can be called Christian only by courtesy. Yet no one will venture to express a doubt that the message of Christ is more necessary to the world today than at any earlier period in our history." (In the volume of addresses, *No Friendly Voice*, p. 137.) The Church does not claim omniscience, and its work has been imperfectly performed, for the Church is human; but it has been the one voice that has persisted through the ages in its witness to the way of justice and love and peace which is given in the Christian gospel.

2. The second function of the Church is to aid men in worship. "Upon this earth there is no scene more impressive," writes Joseph Fort Newton, "than a company of human souls, or many or few, bowed in the hushed awe of a house of God" (*Things I Know in Religion*, p. 87). There is no higher exercise of the human spirit than that of worship. Here man visions the unseen and lifts his soul in adoration. Here he renews the depleted forces of the spirit and wins strength for life. Here the soul, beaten and bruised, finds healing. Here, in quiet recollection of spirit, we not only see God but look at life once more in the light of the Eternal, find where its true wealth lies, and reaffirm our loyalty to high ends. It is not easy to worship. The tides of daily life do not carry us in this direction. To see the unseen and to live by it is a never-ending challenge. In principle all life should be a sacrament of God; in practice we all need help in order to carry God into life. The Church is a fellowship of worship. All its other service will avail little if it fails in this great task of making God real and of sending men forth with a new sense of his

presence. There is a place for solitude and meditation and individual prayer; but nothing can take the place of the worship of the company, where the common praise and prayer and confession of faith unite us with each other and lift us together, where the word of truth from God is honestly spoken, and the windows of the house of worship look out upon the world to which we are to return with new strength of purpose.

3. The Church stands for service. Religion is possible without service, but not the Christian religion. The room cannot remain dark once it has opened its windows to the light; the life cannot remain self-centered when it has received the God of love. A Christian Church without service would be a contradiction in terms. There is not one interest or need of man that is foreign to the Church. Some of these needs it will meet directly through its own organization and activities, but in increasing measure it should serve the community and the nation through individuals and agencies that it inspires. In times past education, philanthropy, hospitals and healing, drama and recreation, music and art, and even direction of industry have all fallen to its task. But whatever the form taken, nothing human must be alien to it, and it must always remain "the union of those who love in the service of those who need." What its task is in the social order will be further noted in the discussion of social salvation.

4. The ministry of reconciliation is especially needed today. The Church is not only a fellowship, but is the world's great creator of fellowship. Consider first the need of overcoming division. Ours is

a divided world—class against class, race against race, nation against nation; and division means death. The wise leaders of political, industrial, and international life see this, but have not found a way out. Our leagues and courts and pacts are noble efforts but largely futile because unsupported by deeper unifying forces. The Church, so far as it is loyal to the spirit of Christ, rises above these divisions; it knows not white or black, rich or poor. But it does more; it is a creative force for fellowship. It binds men in a brotherhood that reaches round the world and takes in every race. It unites them in a common faith: one God and Father of whom all men are children. Its supreme word is love, and love means fellowship. Paul saw the new force at work in his day, a day that had close resemblance to our own. Christ, he declared, had broken down the middle wall of partition and made men one. When men found him, they found a unity in which there could be "neither Jew nor Greek, neither male nor female, neither bond nor free" (Ephesians 2. 14; Galatians 3. 28). Reverence for all men as brothers and as children of one Father, faith in God and recognition of his authority over all, a spirit of good will uniting us in effort for a common good and cutting across all lines of class and nation—these alone can overcome the divisions that are today making for destruction. These must come through religion and religion must work through the Church.

It is what the Church does that gives it its claim upon men. We need the Church in our own individual life. "Every man who learns what the true goal of life is," says the philosopher Josiah Royce, "must live this twofold existence—as a separate individual—yet also as a member of a spiritual communion which, if loyal, he loves, and in which, in so far as he is loyal, he knows that his only true life is hidden and lived" (*The Problem of Christianity,* Vol. I, p. 203). "This twofold existence" is really one; neither side is possible without the other. We must achieve individual life, rich, strong, free; but life cannot be achieved in a social vacuum, least of all the high life of religion. Many who imagine themselves quite independent of the Church are living on what they have received from the Church, directly through home and early training, indirectly through ideals and institutions, through literature and men who have been molded by the influences of religion mediated through the Church. Life on the highest plane demands fellowship even more than on the lower levels.

But to stop here would be distinctly selfish. What right have we to judge the Church simply in terms of what it can give us, to pass it by because we think the preaching is not great, or the music good, or the social opportunities large? Of course the Church is imperfect, but that very fact constitutes a claim upon us. We may say with Royce: "The true Church is still a sort of ideal challenge to the faithful, rather than an already finished institution." The churches as they are now are not indispensable; but mankind cannot get along without the Church. The Church that serves men has a right to ask that men serve the Church. Individualistic philosophy and the selfish attitude have no more place in religion than anywhere else in life.

IV. THE CHURCH AND THE CHURCHES

So far we have been speaking of the Church, the fellowship of the followers of Jesus Christ. What now shall we say about the churches? For what we actually have is not one Church but many churches. Not merely are there different associations in different countries and communities, but in each locality we find separate and sometimes hostile groups each calling itself a Christian Church. We face the curious paradox here, that the institution which represents the principle of unity, or fellowship, in actual practice appears as division. At a time when the forces of evil are stronger, better organized, and more threatening than ever, the Church is unable to present a united front. It has no common witness in the word that it speaks. It does not know how to unite for action. In a given community one can see a half dozen weak groups using up their resources in the struggle to keep alive, instead of employing them to face common foes and serve community needs. Further, by such divisions the fellowship itself is impoverished; the individual communion is deprived of elements that would enrich its life, becoming instead narrow, sectarian, and parochial.

One of the great tasks of today, therefore, is to work for larger Christian unity. That is being attempted in many different ways, and it would be a great mistake to assume that there is but one way in which it is to be done and one form which it is to take. There is, for example, the idea that there must be one big organization, with one authority, one form of creed, one kind of orders and organization. This is the position of those who, like the Roman Catholics, hold the institutional conception of Christianity. According to this, there can be only one true Church, and the way to unity is to have all Christians submit to this. But that is begging the question, for the real issue is, What is Christianity? What is the Church? Much the same position is held by those for whom Christianity is, first of all, a set of doctrines to be accepted by all as a condition of fellowship. These are really methods of exclusion, not of inclusion, of division and not of unity. Christian unity does not necessarily mean one great organization, and it certainly does not mean uniformity. The Church of the first generation certainly showed no such uniformity or central authority. The Pauline churches, for example, were never administered by the apostles in Jerusalem.

Whatever form the coming unity will take, it must leave room for the first demand of religion, that a man shall be true to himself and to the light that he receives. It must be a unity within which there is liberty. Clearly, too, there must be a certain autonomy in different lands and communities. The task, then, is to secure unity of spirit, the practice of fellowship in life and worship, and a united and cooperative activity.

It is well also to consider how much of actual unity there is among Christians today. First, we all belong to one fellowship of faith and love and life. A large majority of Christians use the Apostles' Creed with its declaration, "I believe in the holy Catholic Church." "Catholic" comes from a Greek word, *holos,* which means "whole." Its use goes back to a time when there was no division of "Catholic" and Protestant, of Eastern and Western Churches. "Holy," as here used, does not mean morally perfect; it means belonging to God. We are all members of one universal fellowship, the Church that belongs to God from which no authority of men can shut us out. We are, first of all, not Presbyterians or Methodists or Roman Catholics, but Christians and members of this Church of God, the Church that takes in every land, that goes back through history and unites us in fellowship with Paul and Peter, with Augustine and Francis of Assisi, with John Huss and Martin Luther, with John Calvin, John Wesley, and John Fox. Further, that which unites the different Christian groups is much greater than that which divides. What have I in common, for example, with the devout men and women in the Roman Catholic Church? We believe in one God and in one Lord Jesus Christ; they accept all those books of the Bible which I use, though they add certain others of a secondary rank, the apocrypha; we are agreed that the highest way of life is to live according to the spirit of Christ; like them, I hope that some time that spirit shall rule in all the life of men; together we hope for a life to come in the presence of God.

It is well also to note what is actually being done to advance unity today. The World Conference on Faith and Order has brought together all Christian bodies except the Roman Church, as has the Universal Christian Council for Life and Work. Great mission gatherings like the Jerusalem Conference have back of them increasing co-operation in the mission fields and at home. The United Church of Canada, in which

Presbyterians, Methodists, and Congregationalists have joined, and Methodist union in America are prominent illustrations of continual progress in organic union. The Federal Council of the Churches of Christ in America, representing practically all Protestant communions, is a fine illustration of co-operative effort. But the list is far too long to enumerate. Mutual understanding that will remove prejudice and further fellowship, a larger insight into the nature of Christianity as spiritual and not institutional, increasing fellowship and co-operation within present conditions, and, above all, a richer religious life—these are the great needs if we are to have larger Christian unity.

QUESTIONS FOR DISCUSSION

The principal forms of service which the Church should render to the individual; to a community.

What has been the service of the Church in history?

What charges can be made against the Church in regard to failure in duty or harmful attitudes and actions?

State in order the forms of help which you would like to receive from the Church.

What is the obligation of the individual in relation to the Church as regards membership, attendance, and service?

What are the essential elements which go to make up a Christian Church?

FOR FURTHER READING

Articles in *E. R. E.*, Hastings' *D. B.*, and *The Catholic Encyclopedia*

William Adams Brown: *The Church, Catholic and Protestant*

B. H. Streeter, Editor: *The Spirit*, Chaps. IV, V

Frederick C. Grant: *Frontiers of Christian Thinking*

F. G. Peabody: *The Church of the Spirit*

H. F. Rall: *A Working Faith*

XVIII

THE LIFE TO COME

I. TIME AND THE ETERNAL

IF a man die, shall he live again? That is the question that has haunted men for ages. We do not think of it much in youth, for then life seems to stretch endlessly before us and time means simply new opportunity. It is when the years pass that we see, as the ancients did, that time is the all destroyer, devouring all her children; that nothing seems secure, whether the works of man's hands, the objects of his love, his hope of high achievement, or his own existence.

We are dealing here with a bigger question than that of individual survival after death; it is the problem of time and the Eternal, of change and the enduring. Paul saw it as the problem of the seen and the unseen. "For the things which are seen are temporal; but the things which are not seen are eternal." Often it has been conceived as the question of this world and the next. What we think about the future life, then, must have as its background the question about these two worlds and their relation to each other.

Otherworldliness is one answer to this question. Primitive Christianity showed a good deal of this otherworldly temper. "Our citizenship is in heaven," wrote Paul. "The world passeth away, and the lusts thereof," we read in John. In part the explanation of this lay in the fact that they believed that this age was at its end, that in a little while the Lord would return and the new age would begin. When Jesus did not thus return in visible form and the world went on its old way, the influence of this apocalypticism waned, but other influences entered to cause men to depreciate this life and center their thought on the life to come. Christianity was profoundly affected by a dualism that was Oriental and Hellenistic, rather than coming from the Old Testament or Jesus. Men believed in a world of the spirit, pure and unchanging, which existed above the world of time. The material was evil, or at least worthless. So asceticism came in to support otherworldliness. Men spoke of "these vile bodies," and sang "this world's a wilderness of woe, this world is not my home." One must remember, too, that for vast numbers of men life was a hard and constant struggle against hunger and disease, so this world became a place from which to escape, and religion moved largely around the fear of hell and hope of heaven.

In sharp contrast, the modern age is marked by this-worldliness. The change began with the Renaissance. The humanists of that age did not deny the other world, but they insisted upon the claims of this, upon the freedom of the mind to explore and know, upon man's right to enjoy the beauties and values of this life. Modern science followed. It changed man's attitude to the world from one of helplessness and fear to one of knowledge and mastery. With the tools that it furnished man attacked the job of making this world a good place in which to live, multiplying its comforts and pleasures. More and more man's whole view of the world and life was affected. A naturalistic philosophy saw this world as the only real world;

a secularistic way of life saw this world's goods as the only objects of interest and value.

Christian thought has come to a truer understanding of these two worlds and their relation. It is neither this-worldly or other-worldly. It refuses to set matter against spirit, time against the eternal, this world against the next. This world is not evil or meaningless. We are not to hate it or flee it, or, Stoiclike, merely to endure it. There is an order for us to learn, a beauty to admire. Food and drink, strength of body and faculties of mind, the normal interests and appetites of body and spirit, the varied human fellowships, all are good for us to enjoy.

But Christian thought declares that no man can either understand this world or enjoy it aright unless he sees it in the light of the other. Time must be understood in the setting of the eternal—not an eternal that is far off, a world above or an age beyond, but an eternal that is here and now. The tragedy of those who see only this world is that they miss this world as well as the other. Only the eternal can give meaning to time. It alone can make us masters instead of slaves, deliver us from fear, and give us security and courage and strength. We enjoy each material gift doubly because we take it from God. We are not dependent upon it, because we have the gifts and resources of the spirit. We do not over-value these things, because religion gives us perspective. And we know how to make these things serve the higher ends.

The great word, then, is not "Present" or "Future"; it is the Eternal which takes in both now and then. But if we believe thus in a world of the Eternal, a world of spirit, of supreme values and reality, then two other considerations follow. (1) There is a judgment upon this world which we must acknowledge. Evil forces are here as well as good. Time and change continually destroy. The world of time cannot be the last word of a good God. Hence (2) the ground for our belief in another and enduring world, a world in which the good here achieved shall be secure and the highest good waits to be achieved. In the purpose of God this world plays its significant part, but that purpose must include more for his finite creation than what we see about us.

II. Faith in the Life Eternal

What is the Christian belief in immortality and on what grounds is it held? The most common mistake in discussing belief in the future life is to imagine that it can be considered by itself. But whether we consider what immortality means or why we hold it, we must see it in the larger setting already indicated. No discussion of the "indestructibility of the soul," no "demonstrations" of spiritualism by themselves can determine this matter. A doctrine of immortality can only be reached on the basis of our total belief about God and the world.

Faith in immortality is not mere belief in continued existence after death. It is not existence but life with which we are here concerned, not mere duration but quality. "To believe in immortality is one thing," wrote Robert Louis Stevenson, "but, first of all, it is needful that we believe in life." Eternal life rather than immortality expresses the Christian faith. It is not a matter, first of all, of life after death. Man's life is eternal when he enters into a living relation with the eternal world, that is, with God; and this life may be here and now. This is the theme of the fourth Gospel: "He that believeth hath eternal life. . . . And this is life eternal, that they should know thee the only true God" (John 6. 47; 17. 3). Christianity's interest is in achieving life, not preserving existence. Mere existence as such has no value; but if it is without meaning here, why be concerned about it in the hereafter?

Here lies the inadequacy of spiritualism. It is the claim of spiritualism that it lifts the whole matter of the future life from mere speculation and wishful thinking to a scientific level, that it demonstrates the fact of individual survival by communications of a physical kind with those who have died. We may here pass by the examination of such proofs, remembering only how easy deception is in this field. The important point is that even if such communication be conceded, the real question is not settled. Spiritualism at most would only prove some kind of conscious existence for some indefinite period of time. Why should such an existence have any more meaning in another world than it has in this? Something more is needed. The center about which spiritualism revolves is the soul and its survival; the center about which Christianity revolves is God, God and the meaning which life has through faith in God.

III. The Grounds for Our Belief

Clearly it follows from all this that the final and supreme ground for belief in the future life is belief in God. The whole question comes at last to this:

What is the ultimate reality in this world, matter or spirit, things or God? And is this God good, is this Spirit personal, one who knows us and cares? If there is a God like this, then that is secure which we cherish most highly—truth, love, righteousness, friends; and these are secure, not just now, but forever. They have come into being in this world of time, but they belong to the Eternal. The question is not settled by looking at man, by asking about the indestructibility of the soul, or bringing up analogies from nature about spring that follows winter and life that renews itself from death. We must believe in God if we are to believe in immortality. Tennyson begins his "In Memoriam" at the right point, with the God of power who is also just.

> "Thine are these orbs of light and shade;
> Thou madest life in man and brute;
> Thou madest Death; and lo, thy foot
> Is on the skull which thou hast made.

> "Thou wilt not leave us in the dust;
> Thou madest man, he knows not why;
> He thinks he was not made to die;
> And thou hast made him: thou art just."

With such a God, there follows a conception of man which also points the way to immortality. To some it seems presumptuous that man should single himself out among the myriad creatures great and small as alone worthy of survival, and absurd to see in man the one exception to a seemingly universal law of decay and death. But the situation is different if we begin with God and his purpose instead of with man. The God whom we find through Jesus Christ is Creative Good Will, giving life to his crea-

tures. The highest form of that life which we know
is a creature who can enter into fellowship with God,
can share his spirit, know his high ends, and work
with him. Not all men reach this level, but that is
God's goal. There may be other and like creatures
elsewhere in the universe. And there may be, nay
must be, higher reaches of life for humanity to
achieve, especially in its social expression; but this
would seem to be the highest plane: life which can
share the mind and spirit of God. If God intended
man for this fellowship, if he thus lifts man up to a
union of love and purpose with himself, then man
cannot be "cast as rubbish to the void." A Father
cannot thus let his children perish.

To this argument from faith in God and in man,
we may turn to the consideration of faith in a rational universe. In our study of the grounds for
belief in God we considered the double rationality
of the universe: the rationality of ground or cause,
and that of purpose or end. In science we assume
the former: an orderly world in which nothing happens without some adequate ground. Without this
there could be no science, no certainty in action, no
life at all. The other kind of rationality has to do
with ends, or values. It is the conviction that the
world has meaning as well as order, that there are
ends being achieved. Without this there could be no
moral or religious life. As a matter of fact, our
universe actually has produced, and does produce,
beauty and goodness and other high values. If this
is all an accident, if there is in all this neither
thought nor purpose, then we are in a cosmic madhouse. A universe where the course of events is

without purpose is as crazy as one where events occur without cause. But if there be reason and purpose in the world, then human immortality becomes probable. A rational universe must not only create values, it must preserve them; and values live only in personal beings, in beings that can see beauty and know truth and achieve goodness in character and life. What kind of universe would it be, then, which would produce all this only to let it perish? Look at the picture as it would be in such a case: Ages of slow evolution have brought forth here on earth, and perhaps in other spheres, creatures who can know and love and aspire, in whom moral and spiritual values are realized. But these must all perish, one by one, and then the race itself, till only death and darkness remain. We must face, then, the choice: either we hold to immortality or this universe is irrational and

> "earth is darkness at the core,
> And dust and ashes all that is."

We say, then, with Emerson: "What is excellent, as God lives, is permanent."

One important consideration remains to be stated: It takes more than an intellectual exercise to give a vital belief in immortality. Men become certain of eternal life only by entering in upon it; you must experience it and practice it if you are to believe in it. The first matter is to be sure of God, to know the powers of this world of the spirit which time and change and death cannot affect. It is when spiritual life ebbs that men lose faith in immortality. It is when men know the reality and power of this higher world that, with Paul, they become certain that "neither death, nor life, nor angels, nor principalities, nor things present, nor things to come, nor height, nor depth, nor any other creature, shall be able to separate" them from the love of God.

IV. SOME QUESTIONS AND OBJECTIONS

Is the belief in immortality selfish? No. Men do not usually become interested in the future life through concern for themselves, but only when death takes those whom they love deeply or greatly admire. Faced with this situation, they cannot believe that such spirits, with all their love and faith and courage, become in a moment nothing more than the dust of the street, that their lives have no more abiding meaning than the swarms of ephemeridae who flutter a few hours above the sands and lie lifeless the next morning. Faith in immortality is the brave protest of the spirit against the idea that lives like this are at the mercy of brute force and blind change. But the individual interest in immortality may itself be the fine expression of a noble spirit which has learned the secret of life in faith and service and finds it good. So we can applaud Dr. Wilfred Grenfell as he writes, not from the comforts of London, but from bleak Labrador: "I am very much in love with life. I want all I can get of it. I want more of it, after the incident called death, if there is any to be had" (quoted by W. Cosby Bell, *If a Man Die*, p. 51).

How can the spirit survive when the body is destroyed? Is not the mind at every point dependent upon the body? Thus we know that the failure of a single endocrine gland to function properly may mean an otherwise normal child developing into semi-idiocy, and that the most remarkable return to normal mind and body conditions can be secured by supplying the deficiency.

But there are other important facts to be taken into account. The powerful influence of the mind upon the body is equally plain. It may produce sickness, it may promote health. Under special excitement of mind men have done what was impossible in normal conditions. What is more, while the body is necessary for the development of the self, yet the mind seems to grow more independent of the body. As soon as a man reaches maturity the body begins to decline; we literally begin to die at thirty. But the mind may move on with steady growth even beyond threescore and ten, and the flame of the spirit burn clear and bright, as with a Wesley, when the body is frail from age and ready to break down. All this suggests a different conception, that the body is not the cause but the setting and condition for the growth of the spirit, that the spirit may become more and more independent of the body till the latter is discarded as the scaffolding which comes down when the real structure has been reared.

Let us remember too that the Christian hope is not that of the life of a disembodied spirit. The idea of a literal physical resurrection is widely given up. But Paul's idea of a "spiritual body" is another matter. We cannot say what such a body may be like. The body here on earth is the means by which we establish active and fruitful relations with the world about us. To speak of the "resurrection of the body" may be and usually is misleading, but what the term stands for is plain. It means that the next life will be incomparably richer than this, and that we shall not lack the means for contact with our world, for effective action, and for fellowship with others. It is not knowledge, of course, that we have here but simply faith, a confidence based on our convictions as to God.

There is, finally, the objection repeatedly raised in the name of evolution. Matter came first, we are told, mind much later; therefore mind is dependent, incidental, and cannot hope to survive the death of the body. But this is begging the question, not facing it. Of course the rule for the race as for the individual is "first that which is natural, then that which is spiritual," as Paul said long ago. But whether that is the rule for the universe is another matter, and there the real issue lies. Did order and beauty, law and truth, reason and goodness all come from the clash of atoms and the whirl of electrons, or does the universe reveal Creative Spirit slowly working out its ends in a visible world? We have seen reasons for holding the latter, rather than the former with its idea of something out of nothing. But if the latter be true, then this objection falls out. The spirit of man is not a chance and late arrival on the shores of time. It is the final work of that Creative Spirit of which the world of ordered nature as well as of spiritual values bears witness. And if Spirit is basic and ultimate, and not matter, then the human spirit may survive.

V. About Judgment and Hell

So far we have talked about the saints and their

hope of heaven; but what about the sinners and the Church's teaching as to the judgment and hell? And what about the many who, if they have not chosen the way of evil, have yet not found the way of good and the life with God: the ignorant and the careless, the abnormal and subnormal, and those who have lived without privilege and light of truth in dark ages or dark lands? Fortunately, it is not ours to decide all this. Nevertheless, we can at least consider some principles to guide us here and cast out some unchristian ideas that have remained too long in Christian thought.

First of all, judgment is both a fact and a faith. We see the facts round about us. What men sow, they reap. Sin is selfishness arrayed against good will, it is disloyalty in the place of obedience to the highest. Selfishness and disloyalty mean anarchy in the social world and destruction of the individual. There is a judgment on sin that inheres in the very process of life. The nations that are following the ways of selfishness and greed, of militarism and oppression, the history of the World War and of the years since 1918, all bear witness to this judgment. It is the same in individual lives. This is not a doctrine of despair, however, but of hope. Such judgment is essential to a moral universe. Righteousness and truth have the forces of the universe on their side. Evil destroys itself. And there is something more: judgment culminates, it means something at the end of history. In this world good and evil are in the making; they are not only inseparable but are often hardly to be distinguished. But each tends more and more to move on to its completion. The completion of good is the heaven of God; the completion of sin is the judgment on sin. And there will be an inevitable final separation as each goes to its own.

To hold this does not mean to accept all that has been said in the past as to hell. Ours is no vindictive, vengeful God; he has no joy in suffering. Punishment is not something inflicted from without; it is the working out of the consequence of sin. Hell is life separated from God and good, defeated, frustrated, self-destroyed; and we see it here and now. Flames no more make hell than walls and streets make heaven. We need to be especially careful not to be dogmatic or omniscient about how this judgment is to take place. Judgment is not as simple as our theologies have made it. We must face the fact that men cannot so easily be divided into saints and sinners. Human life is in the making. How many saints are there, clear in faith, ripe in character, and ready for heaven? How many sinners are there who are irrevocably fixed in evil and given to sin? And what of the immature, the unprivileged, and the rest?

We are not trying to take God's place as judge, but simply to understand. Clearly, some of our ideas must be revised. One mistake is thinking of life as a mere probation, a putting men on trial before they are judged. No, this world is not so much a place for the testing as for the making of men; that is God's great concern. And why should he be limited to this world? The physical fact of death does not at a stroke change these mixed and unformed lives into pure saints or sinners. If the world to come has place for growth and change, that may mean change of direction. We cannot believe that a Christlike God will ever turn away from men who turn to him, or cease in his effort to win men from death to life.

At the same time there are other facts which we must face. (1) Character tends toward increasing fixity. All life is a choosing of what we will be; there is no desire, no word, no deed that does not register itself, and the result is at once our choice and our destiny. (2) There is a law of spiritual gravitation by which the good and the evil both move toward their own kind and their own place. (3) Sin necessarily, by its very nature as well as its desire, means separation from God. And this is essentially what hell means: it is separation from God, the evil which men choose as their life, and the fellowship of those who are evil like themselves.

Questions for Discussion

How does faith in eternal life differ from belief in existence after death?

What are the chief grounds for belief in immortality stated in order of importance?

What are the chief obstacles to such belief in the modern mind?

Does belief in the eternal tend to minimize or destroy for men the significance and value of the temporal and historical, or to heighten them?

For Further Reading

John Baillie: *And the Life Everlasting*
W. Cosby Bell: *If a Man Die*
B. H. Streeter, Editor: *Concerning Immortality*
Harry Emerson Fosdick: *The Assurance of Immortality*
A. S. Pringle-Pattison: *The Idea of Immortality*
J. Y. Simpson: *Man and the Attainment of Immortality*
J. H. Leckie: *The World to Come and Final Destiny*
W. R. Inge and others: *What Is Hell?*

XIX

A SOCIAL FAITH

I. The Social Need

THERE is one question which no one can escape today who has any concern for his fellow men. We call it, somewhat vaguely, the social problem. By social life we mean the life of men in their group relations; home, industry, church, and state are the main forms, but it includes many other relations—recreation, education, international relations, life anywhere where men think and feel and act together.

About this group life we must note two facts. First, it was never so close and so inclusive as today. Science, invention, and industry are responsible for the change. Science brought in the power machine. The machine meant mass production, concentrated capital and control, and masses of people brought together in great centers. At the same time invention was breaking down distance and other barriers that divided men. The means of communication—printing press, telegraph, telephone, radio, movie, telephoto, and television—and the means of transportation—railway, steamship, automobile, airplane, and submarine—these have radically changed the group life of men. The world has become one family. What happens in New York today is read tomorrow in Tokio and Peiping, Calcutta and Cairo, Melbourne and Buenos Ayres, or the radio may take it within a few hours to countless millions. Humanity is becoming more and more one big organism, a body that flashes to the center each experienced emotion, which in turn is sent back and felt through the whole frame. Recently one Indian prince decided to set up a radio with loud speaker in each of his villages. Tomorrow his forty million people will become one body in a new sense.

Even more important for us to face is the second fact: though bound together as never before, we have not learned to live together; our differences and conflicts, indeed, have been multiplied, and the very closeness of the ties has made more tragic the results. We have had marvelous tools put into our hands, but we have not known how to use them. (1) Our inventions have become means of destruction so terrible that we hardly dare to think what another world war might mean. (2) Our instruments of production have resulted in an industry which men have used for individual profit instead of for feeding and clothing men. So, just at the time when we could mine coal, make clothing and shoes, and produce food in such abundance as never before, we saw, instead of happy, busy, and well-cared-for peoples, everywhere around the world folks that were hungry, half-clothed, and with no chance to work. (3) Our means of travel and trade and communication, despite some growth of unity, have brought a vast increase of tension and strife, so that war is most imminent at the very time when it is most terrible in its possibilities. Press and radio are used, not to secure mutual understanding, but for world-wide propaganda, for suppressing truth, distorting facts, and stirring up fears and hatreds. The press in most countries is the subservient tool of the State, and the European news agencies are mainly State-owned or controlled. In many cases, especially in our cities, the daily press is just one more form of big business, with enormous investment, used openly or covertly to further special interests in politics or economics. Everywhere we find class against class, race against race, nation against nation. Humanity, with this enormous technical development, is like a boy suddenly grown to manhood in physical strength and passions, but mentally and morally still a child.

II. THE RELEVANCY OF RELIGION

What can religion do about this?

There are those who think that religion has no relevancy here. (1) Some of these speak for business and the State, and call to the Church, "Hands off!" Their theory is simple: Business and the State will attend to this world, let the Church attend to the next. Let the concern of religion be with what happens inside the four walls of the church, not outside. Let it bring men comfort and hope. Let it preach the "pure gospel." Let it point men to heaven. But let those whose business it is attend to industry and the State. Many such men will give financial support to churches; but they want an individual and otherworldly religion and ministers who will keep silence on social matters. Within their own field they demand supremacy. The Fascist State is only the outstanding expression of this position. (2) Some men take this position on religious grounds. They declare that the world is evil, and our task is not to change this world but to save men out of this world.

Or they insist that religion is individual, not social, concerned not with "outer life," but wholly with the inner and "spiritual."

But religion cannot accept any such limitations. Neither the Old Testament nor the New presents us with a merely individualistic or otherworldly religion. There is one God, and he is the Lord of all life. No *Duce* or *Führer,* no King or Congress, no business association or editor has any authority over against him. We have only one hope—that in this world and all worlds his will is to be done and his rule is to come. Because we believe in the one "God, the Father Almighty," we must claim all life for religion. The religion of a corner, the religion of a mere segment of life, is impossible. It must be all or nothing.

III. INDIVIDUAL AND SOCIAL

A great deal of confusion has come because men have set individual and social over against each other. One side pleads for a "social gospel," the other for individual religion. There is, of course, a distinction between individual and social. There is an inner life, a world within each man, a microcosm, a center of conscious being and purpose which forever marks off each individual from all others. And there is a social life, a group life that we share together. But these are not two kinds of life and they do not indicate two kinds of religion or two gospels.

It is just as impossible to separate spiritual and physical, and bid religion care for the former and pass the latter by. Religion is concerned with man and man is a unity. When Toyohiko Kagawa went to live in the slum district of Shinkawa, he turned to

the little children to win them for a better life, and
they responded quickly and gladly. Then he had
to look on and see them, as they grew up, overborne
by their evil surroundings. "Because of insufficient
income half of the children were undernourished and
died before they reached the age of five. . . . Those
about him resorted to drink in order to paralyze their
brains and nerves and forget their suffering."
(*Kagawa,* by William Axling, pp. 44-48.) The
boys turned to vice and crime, the girls to prostitu-
tion. He saw that he must liberate the laborer in
order to save the slums. He kept on with his preaching and evangelizing, but he organized the first labor
union in Japan and later began his work with co-
operatives. Religion, says Kagawa, is "an art concerned with the whole of life. . . . It is only the timid
who interpret God and the world as a dualism. Until
even the Stock Exchange is filled to saturation with
God, there is little hope for genuine religion." How
can we build up men and women in lives of faith and
high ideals and unselfish love and service, when the
tides of the society in which they live and work move
constantly, deep and strong, in the direction of materialism, selfishness, and ruthless struggle?

Human life is always both individual and social,
and human life as a whole is what religion is interested in. There is no merely individual being. What
is society? It is men living, thinking, working together, with certain common attitudes and ideals.
What is the individual? He is a conscious center of
life, but one whose actual living, in terms of what he
does and feels and thinks, is mainly in a life shared
with others. No individual could ever reach a human,

personal life except in the social matrix; and the higher he rises, the more indispensable do the social relations become.

IV. WE NEED SOCIAL SALVATION

The first point that we need to see clearly is that group life has moral and religious qualities and capacities, and that it is more than a mere sum of individuals in action. We are dealing once more with the idea of the organic, or corporate. The whole is more than the sum of its parts; corporate life and individual life each depend upon the other, but there is such a thing as corporate life. There is a life that we live together as well as one that we live individually. This common life, as seen in home or state or business, is no mere impersonal affair of laws and institutions. Here, just as in individual life, we have ideas and ideals, impulses and emotions, high ends or low, evil passions, noble achievements, sins, failures. It is personal and ethical life, like the life of the individual, and, like that, it needs to be saved.

Next to the family, the modern State is perhaps the most significant illustration of such a social, or corporate, entity. The nation of today is really a modern development. It has its traditions, its ideals, often a developed cult of nation worship or glorification that is religious in character, especially where Fascist ideology has come in. It includes more than the political life, though the functions of the political State are enormously extended today and its molding action is felt in every part of the life of the people. The life of the nation has distinct moral quality. It may easily be vain, oversensitive, arrogant, selfish, materialistic, predatory, ruthless. The history of modern nations shows all of these sins. Clearly, the State must be redeemed if a new life is to be achieved for humanity. It must repent of its sins, set new and higher goals, and change its spirit and method. It must find a new faith, faith in God, faith in the forces of truth and justice and good will. It must acknowledge a supreme authority, recognizing that it has the right to rule only so far as it has itself learned to obey.

The basic ideals of the world of industry as organized under present-day capitalism are largely non-Christian. Christianity holds to an idea of stewardship, or trusteeship: this earth and all its goods, its fields and mines and factories, belong to God. Man has no title in fee simple but only in trust; and he is to use all possessions for the good of men. Our present system thinks in terms of absolute control; if a man, by inheritance or in any other way, commands a fortune or owns a million acres or controls a hundred factories, no one is to question his right to do with it as he pleases, though ten thousand men are shut out from the land and a job. Christianity emphasizes brotherhood as a fact, an ideal, and a practice. It stands for justice, not as a mere system of rewards and punishment, but as a creative social effort to secure the largest opportunity and the fullest share of the gifts of life for all. And in the light of all this it holds up the service of men as a motive in life. Our present system stresses individualism, appeals to selfish interest, and measures a man's success by the wealth and power which he has secured for himself. Christianity stresses the solidarity of humanity, that the good life for each can only come with the good of all; and so it stands for the method of co-operation. Our industrial system today is built upon the competitive principle, and even where there is common effort, as within an organized labor group, a corporation, or even a nation, it is still directed against other interests or groups or nations. So careful a writer as J. M. Keynes, a capitalist economist, is driven to say: "Modern capitalism is absolutely irreligious, without internal union, without much public spirit, often, though not always, a mere congeries of possessors and pursuers." (Quoted by Sherwood Eddy, in *Russia Today*, p. 239.) The question here is not that of the spirit and attitude of men working under this system, but of the ideals underlying the system and the methods involved in it.

If we turn to international life, we see once more a world in which a new group life has arisen, where no longer any nation can live by itself, but where this common life has been shaped in the main along anti-Christian lines. We cannot deny the statement once made by Viscount Bryce that the nations in relation to each other are still in a "state of nature," that is, still essentially in the barbarian stage. It is true that we have in international relations the beginnings of a new order, with mutual regard, co-operation, the settlement of questions in open conference, and the avowed aim of justice. But the actual events of the generation just passed reveal as dominant factors secret agreements, groups of hostile interests arrayed against each other, frankly selfish aims, and dependence upon armed force. Nationalism, secret diplomacy, and militarism are the characteristic marks of our national-international system, and all three are as flatly opposed to the Christian ideal as they are to human welfare. Nationalism sets the interests of each State against that of other States and claims for the State an absolute authority without regard to justice, truth, or God. Diplomacy in actual practice means deceit as a method and the arraying of one group of nations against another as a policy. War is the very essence of the spirit of anti-Christ. There is not one high ideal for which Christianity stands which must not be scrapped when war is on. Against love and truth and mercy and peace and reverence for humanity, it sets hate, deception, hard vindictiveness, violence, and murder, making of men tools for ambition and food for cannon. All that we denounce in individual men—lying, anger, murder—is sanctified in the conduct of nations when war arises.

Of course there is individual action and responsibility in all this, but there is more. Here is corporate life. Here are group sins that must be confessed and repented of by the group, ideals that must be transformed, institutions that must be made over. That is what social salvation means.

V. What Has Christianity to Offer?

What has the Christian religion to offer for this needed transformation?

1. Christianity offers a goal. The Christian term is "the kingdom of God," better translated, "the rule of God." The prophets looked at a world in which evil held sway. (As men of faith they could have but one answer to such a situation: Sometime oppression

and cruelty and poverty and war shall cease, the forces of evil be overthrown, and the rule of God shall come. Jesus struck the same note: "The rule of God is at hand." There are two ways of conceiving this rule. One is to think of it as external, as a rule of compelling force, autocratic and irresistible, and of God as external to his world and as a kind of Oriental King. The other way is to think of an inner rule, with ideals that command mind and conscience, and a spirit that sways the heart while at the same time it reaches out to shape and master all life, physical and spiritual, individual and social, with all the institutions of business and government. The prophets and Jesus and Paul thought of the kingdom as such an inner yet all-determining rule.

The late Lord Chief Justice Russell of England, who was of Irish stock, once gave a noteworthy definition of civilization: "It is not dominion, wealth, material luxury; nay, not even a great literature and education widespread, good though these may be. Civilization is not a veneer; it must penetrate to the very heart and core the societies of men. Its true signs are thought for the poor and suffering, chivalrous regard and respect for woman, the frank recognition of human brotherhood irrespective of race or color or nation or religion, the narrowing of the domain of mere force as a governing factor in the world, abhorrence of what is mean and cruel and vile, ceaseless devotion to the claims of justice." Here the influence of the Christian ideal is obvious.

Let us note some of the principles which will come to expression in this new world. (1) The sacredness of man as man. It is not Nordic blood that decides, not color of skin, or race, or degree of culture; it is man as man to whom these rights belong. And the goal and test of all industry and government is what it does for man. (2) Justice, not of the courts, distributing according to deed, but as the quality of a social order which gives the largest opportunity of life to least and greatest. (3) Good will as the ruling spirit, an active, creative attitude alike of men and nations, working for the good of all. (4) The principle of solidarity, mankind as one, and the highest welfare of each as gained only in and through the common life. (5) Co-operation as the social way and service as the great motive. That would mean what Tawney has called a "functional society" in contrast with our present "acquisitive society," a society in which "the main object of social emphasis would be the performance of social functions," and "which inquired first not what men possess but what they can make or create or achieve." It is obvious that this kingdom of God is not a mere matter of authority or organization; Paul uses for it the figure of a body, Jesus of a family. It is a corporate life.

2. Christianity offers the necessary authority. The indispensable conditions of a strong and enduring society are a common faith and a common authority. Today we have industrial and international anarchy because the dominant social order recognizes no motive except self-interest, and no authority beyond that of wealth and force. A common and higher authority can only be found where men believe in God, in some Being that embodies at once goodness and power. H. G. Wells wrote some years ago of an interview in Rome with David Lubin, the far-seeing Jew who es-

tablished the International Institute of Agriculture. It was after the World War, and Wells was insisting that what was needed was the recognition of some God or King that all nations would recognize and in whom all would find a common truth and justice to which they must bow. He told how the old man rose to his feet, walked over to a table and seized the Scriptures of his race: "But I have it here," he cried, "here in the prophets of my people." And David Lubin was right.

3. Christianity offers a needed faith, the faith in a living God, not simply as a supreme and unifying authority, but as a Power working out high ends. Justice and truth and love are not mere words or remote ideals. They have their being in God, they are the finally determining forces of this universe. Here is hope to displace despairing skepticism and nerve us for social action. No matter what today or tomorrow brings, we fight on. For

> "Right is right, since God is God;
> And right the day must win;
> To doubt would be disloyalty,
> To falter would be a sin."

Christianity has faith in man also. Without that we cannot go forward, at least in the democratic way. Christianity is not romanticism, seeing only good in man; it faces realistically the dark side of human nature. But it is not cynical or pessimistic; it believes, not in man as he is, but in man's capabilities, in what man can be as God works in him and through him. Therefore, looking forward to a new and better world, it does not rely upon some autocratic "leader" here on earth, or upon a miraculous descent of God from the skies, but upon the slow but sure work of the forces of truth, love, and justice, operative in men.

4. Christianity offers the necessary social dynamic, those forces without which our social plans are beautiful but empty dreams. It transforms individual men, furnishing them with vision and passion, supplying both leaders and followers for the work of social change.

VI. THE CHRISTIAN WAY

What is the way of making over our social order? The answer to this question varies.

1. Apocalypticism is one of the oldest answers. It holds that this world is utterly evil. There is no hope in anything that man can do, but sometime God will come (or the Messiah) and by irresistible power will destroy the evil and establish the good. Premillennialism is the popular form of this idea. It holds that Christ will return in visible form and set up a kingdom in Jerusalem, from which he will rule the whole earth by military power for a thousand years, after which will come a final Judgment and heaven and hell. Karl Barth has revived apocalypticism in Europe. For him the idea of Christianizing our social order is like "biting on granite." The whole world of time and change is evil; when God acts, he will put an end to history and the perfect eternal order will be here.

2. The second method might be called revolutionism. Strictly, every idea of social salvation that is at all thorough must be revolutionary; the early Christians were accused of "turning the world upside down." But here we are using revolutionism for the

theory, especially as held by Communism, that those who profit by the present order can only be dispossessed by force. This Communism is like apocalypticism in may respects. Both hold that the present order cannot be changed gradually, but must grow constantly worse until overturned by force. In apocalypticism God is to use this force; with Communism it is man.

We cannot assert that force is never needed. So long as there are immaturity and ignorance and evil, some constraint and compulsion are needed where the affairs of a group are concerned, and that is true even in the home. The wise mother will snatch a child who is too near the open fire without waiting first for peaceful persuasion. Society has its police, courts, and jails. Coercion need not be physical to be real and potent, and no sharp line can be drawn ethically between violent and non-violent coercion. But the new order which men need and God purposes, though it must in the end control all the outward forms of life, is fundamentally moral and spiritual. And the spiritual cannot be won by physical force. Violence in such case inevitably means compulsion of spirit as well as body. Autocracy is evil whether wielded by one man or by a class, and whether its ends are avowedly benevolent or selfish. Force can destroy, and, indeed, some things need to be destroyed; but mere force cannot build up, for that we must have other agencies. And the use of violence, whether between nations or within a nation, brings inevitably other evils with it. If the sword is to decide, then the supreme appeal is no longer to truth and justice, and these must suffer. We cannot use the weapons of Caesar to bring in the rule of Christ, or expect to rear on the foundations of hatred and violence a kingdom of justice and peace.

3. Over against the appeal to force, whether used by God or man, stands the reliance on the power of the spirit. Truth, the sense of right or justice, and good will are influences on which this method relies. It may be called the democratic way. Those who follow it believe that men, however dull or selfish or ignorant or swayed by prejudice, may be changed, and will at last respond to truth and right. They believe that even the group which profits by the present system may be so influenced. In any case they hold that in countries with democratic institutions, such as Great Britain and the United States, the method of discussion, agitation, education, and orderly political procedure should be used to secure needed change. When the people can be lifted to where they see the true goal, desire it, and are willing to work for it, they can gain it; without that it could not be given them. And, indeed, every generation must win anew for itself such high goods as freedom and justice.

It is clear that this democratic method has a close kinship with Christianity. Its reliance on nonphysical forces, its appeal to conscience and reason, its concern with freedom and justice, all indicate this. Political democracy in its actual working has failed at important points. (1) It has laid too great stress on mere change in laws and institutions, and failed to see that these, to be effective, must express the will and spirit of the people. (2) It has assumed that when once a truth is seen and uttered, the victory has been gained. But the real task is to shape the mind and will of a people. So it has failed at its greatest task, the revolution in the spirit and character of men. It needs more realism in facing the forces of human ignorance, selfishness, prejudice, and inertia. (3) It has failed to see that without industrial democracy, political democracy is of little worth.

4. When we ask about the Christian way of help in the social problem, we are met by two answers.

(1) Our problem lies with the individual, says one group; once get the individual right and government and industry will be transformed. But (a) individual men, who seem to be quite sincere and devout in personal religion, are often quite blind to social sins and social demands. In my files is a letter from a great industrial magnate who wrote me of his benefactions to churches and his interest in religion, making a plea for the gospel of charity. But a few years later, when some workmen went to the office of his company to ask relief from a twelve-hour day and a seven-day week, they were thrown out bodily. The men who summon the Church to stick to the pure gospel and work for individual conversion do not always show a zeal for peace and justice in business and the State. (b) And how are men to be Christians individually when they are socially enmeshed in a pagan order? I watch business men who worship in the church on Sunday and listen to the gospel of life after the spirit of Christ. But from Monday to Saturday they live in a world of sharpest competition and incessant striving for individual advantage. They must show profits to their directors, and they must make good individually. Are these individuals transforming the pagan order or is this

order making pagan the individual? (c) Social redemption does not come automatically. If all the people of this country were to accept the Christian faith tomorrow, we should only be at the beginning of the solution of our social problems. We should still have to ask what the will of God and the good of man demanded, and then begin the long process of making over our social life.

(2) Our problem lies in the institution, says the other group; men are profoundly affected by the order in which they live and our attack must be upon that order. But who will transform that order except the men in whose heart the principles of that new order already exist? And how can such an order live if it is not thus grounded in the people?

The trouble is once more in that false disjunction of individual and social. It is human life that must be changed, and that includes both the individual and the order. We must have new men for a new society, and a new society if men are to be able to lead fully Christian lives. Where sin is, we must call to repentance. Where life is, we must hold up the Christian demand. We must attack the problems of the individual and the group at the same time, that advance in each may further the other.

5. What is the specific function of organized Christianity, that is, of the Church, in relation to this program of social change?

(1) It must hold before men the goal of a new order, a new humanity where good will and peace and justice shall obtain, where men shall be joined in co-operative effort for a common good.

(2) It must keep alive faith in God, a living God

who is working out these ends; and that means faith in spiritual forces as our reliance.

(3) It must promote the study of such problems as government, industry, war, race relations, and international relations, not offering predetermined solutions, but furthering interest and understanding. The Information Service of the Federal Council of Churches is an example of service in this field.

(4) It is not its function to prepare programs of action, to furnish blueprints of a new social order, or to ally itself with specific political parties. It should, rather, welcome the work of socially minded economists, statesmen, social engineers, and business leaders. Christian men, individually and in groups, will naturally ally themselves as citizens with movements that offer the best way to the highest ends.

(5) The Church must always include judgment and the call to repentance in its message. It may not prescribe how the good shall be achieved, but it can never condone evil or be silent in the presence of iniquity. When billions go for arms while millions exist on starvation allowance, when industry operates to bring wealth to a few and leave millions without a chance to work, when class and race hatred are promoted, when nations compel their men to go forth and kill each other, when national selfishness is the avowed national policy, then it must point out evil and pronounce judgment. And it must call to repentance not only the few who are in places of power, but all men everywhere who share in the nation's life and thus in its guilt.

QUESTIONS FOR DISCUSSION

What conditions or forces have brought about the increase in number and in urgency of "social problems"?

With what right and in what sense may we speak of social sins and of social salvation?

What do you consider the outstanding social sins of today, that is, the greatest evils in our group life?

How can Christianity help through its contribution of a social goal and of social dynamic for our day?

Why is a purely individualistic gospel inadequate?

Are there dangers that come with the emphasis on a "social gospel"?

What are the social values inherent in the Christian concepts of God and of man?

What other socially significant Christian concepts would you name?

FOR FURTHER READING

J. C. Bennett: *Social Salvation*

Walter Rauschenbusch: *A Theology for the Social Gospel; Christianizing the Social Order; Christianity and the Social Crisis*

E. F. Scott: *The Kingdom and the Messiah*

H. F. Ward: *Which Way Religion?; Our Economic Morality and the Ethic of Jesus*

F. E. Johnson: *The Church and Society*

E. Stanley Jones: *Christ's Alternative to Communism*

John Lewis and others, Editors: *Christianity and the Social Revolution*. Sixteen writers discuss the relations of Christianity and Communism.

R. Niebuhr: *Does Civilization Need Religion?*

Information Service: Published weekly by the Federal Council of Churches.

INDEX

I. Names

281

II. SUBJECTS

The reference to a Chapter indicates in each case the major source for the subject in question.

284 INDEX